UNDERSTANDING NONPROFIT

FINANCIAL STATEMENTS

THIRD EDITION

BOARDSOURCE®
Building Effective Nonprofit Boards

BY STEVEN BERGER, CPA

Library of Congress Cataloging-in-Publication Data

Berger, Steven H.

Understanding nonprofit financial statements / by Steven Berger. —
3rd ed.

    p. cm.

Includes bibliographical references.

ISBN 1-58686-104-2 (pbk.)

1. Nonprofit organizations–Finance. 2. Nonprofit organizations–Accounting.
3. Financial statements. I. Title.

          HG4027.65.B47 2008

          658.15'12--dc21

                 2008001683

Published by BoardSource
1828 L Street, NW, Suite 900
Washington, DC 20036

BoardSource, formerly the National Center for Nonprofit Boards, is the premier resource for practical information, tools and best practices, training, and leadership development for board members of nonprofit organizations worldwide. Through our highly acclaimed programs and services, BoardSource enables organizations to fulfill their missions by helping build strong and effective nonprofit boards.

BoardSource provides assistance and resources to nonprofit leaders through workshops, training, and our extensive Web site, www.boardsource.org. A team of BoardSource governance consultants works directly with nonprofit leaders to design specialized solutions to meet organizations' needs and assists nongovernmental organizations around the world through partnerships and capacity building. As the world's largest, most comprehensive publisher of materials on nonprofit governance, BoardSource offers a wide selection of books, videotapes, CDs, and online tools. BoardSource also hosts the BoardSource Leadership Forum, bringing together governance experts, board members, and chief executives of nonprofit organizations from around the world.

Created out of the nonprofit sector's critical need for governance guidance and expertise, BoardSource is a 501(c)(3) nonprofit organization that has provided practical solutions to nonprofit organizations of all sizes in diverse communities. In 2001, BoardSource changed its name from the National Center for Nonprofit Boards to better reflect its mission. Today, BoardSource has approximately 11,000 members and has served more than 75,000 nonprofit leaders.

For more information, please visit our Web site, www.boardsource.org, e-mail us at mail@boardsource.org, or call us at 800-883-6262.

Have You Used These BoardSource Resources?

VIDEOS

Meeting the Challenge: An Orientation to Nonprofit Board Service
Speaking of Money: A Guide to Fundraising for Nonprofit Board Members

BOOKS

Exceptional Board Practices: The Source in Action
Managing Conflicts of Interest: A Primer for Nonprofit Boards
Driving Strategic Planning: A Nonprofit Executive's Guide
Taming the Troublesome Board Member
The Nonprofit Dashboard: A Tool for Tracking Progress
Meet Smarter: A Guide to Better Nonprofit Board Meetings
The Nonprofit Policy Sampler, Second Edition
Getting the Best from Your Board: An Executive's Guide to a Successful Partnership
The Nonprofit Board Answer Book — A Practical Guide for Board Members and Chief Executives, Second Edition
The Source: Twelve Principles of Governance That Power Exceptional Boards
The Nonprofit Legal Landscape
Self-Assessment for Nonprofit Governing Boards
Assessment of the Chief Executive
Fearless Fundraising
The Nonprofit Board's Guide to Bylaws
Transforming Board Structure: Strategies for Committees and Task Forces
The Board Building Cycle: Nine Steps to Finding, Recruiting, and Engaging Nonprofit Board Members, Second Edition
Culture of Inquiry: Healthy Debate in the Boardroom
The Board Chair Handbook: Second Edition

THE GOVERNANCE SERIES

1. *Ten Basic Responsibilities of Nonprofit Boards*
2. *Financial Responsibilities of Nonprofit Boards*
3. *Structures and Practices of Nonprofit Boards*
4. *Fundraising Responsibilities of Nonprofit Boards*
5. *Legal Responsibilities of Nonprofit Boards*
6. *The Nonprofit Board's Role in Setting and Advancing the Mission*
7. *The Nonprofit Board's Role in Planning and Evaluation*
8. *How To Help Your Board Govern More and Manage Less*
9. *Leadership Roles in Nonprofit Governance*

For an up-to-date list of publications and information about current prices, membership, and other services, please call BoardSource at 800-883-6262 or visit our Web site at www.boardsource.org.

Contents

List of Boxes

List of Exhibits

Preface

Every board member of a nonprofit organization — whether or not a member of the board's finance committee — is charged by law with minimum responsibilities of financial oversight for that organization. This book is designed to provide board members with the ability to understand the basic financial documents that they will encounter as board members — and to know what types of documents and information to request from the nonprofit's managers. Without these documents and without a full understanding of them, no board member will be able to meet his or her fiduciary responsibilities.

Introduction

Every nonprofit organization exists to provide value and benefits. If it did not, the organization would not attract a clientele, customers, or donors to sustain it. The benefits, which are rendered to the organization's clientele, are called the *value proposition*. Some of the more common ways to measure value are through customer satisfaction, employee satisfaction, operational excellence, community benefits, or financial results.

In each case, the value must be defined and measured. But raw performance data are not enough to provide meaning. There must be some relative comparison so that numbers can be understood in a context that renders them meaningful. These comparisons generally take the form of ratios that are derived from raw data. For example, some of the more important financial ratios that help define value include operating margin percentage, number of days cash on hand, or debt service quotient.

This book concentrates on one major and widely recognized method of measuring value: financial statements and their implications for outcomes. It is organized to maximize a nonprofit board member's understanding of the most important financial elements within his or her organization. At the outset, the book reviews the function of the board in its goal-setting role, which includes financial outcomes. This sets the stage for examining the differences between simple accounting and the board's function in analyzing accounting numbers to portray financial outcomes. Understanding the major elements of the financial statements is the heart of the book, and attention is given to the key ways in which those elements represent the real financial outcomes of the operations performed by the organization's senior management and staff over the relevant time period.

The remainder of the book highlights similarities and differences of interim versus audited financial statements, some very specific ways to use available financial information to fulfill the board's fiduciary responsibilities, and, finally, how to utilize financial information to measure organizational performance.

What should become evident is the relationship between long-term (five- to 10-year) financial plans and short-term (one year) budgets established by the board, and how these are translated into actual operating results portrayed in the interim (monthly or quarterly) financial statements. It should also become clear how interim results relate to the final results reported in the audited financial statements and why any major differences must be taken seriously.

By the conclusion of the book, board members should have a greater ability to appraise and evaluate such things as statements of financial position and statements of cash flow and activities, and to better understand and communicate with the organization's chief executive about the financial outcomes of the organization. This book will also assist the board in working with chief executives to set organizational goals, which the executives are responsible for meeting, and for evaluating the financial aspects of the chief executive's performance.

Included with this book is a CD-ROM that contains sample financial documents and a Microsoft® PowerPoint® presentation on financial practices that can be used at board meetings to improve financial skills. A description of the contents of the CD-ROM is found in Appendix 2.

1.

The Distinct Roles of the Board and the Chief Executive

At the outset, it is important to understand the different roles played by the board and the executive in sound financial management. The board is ultimately responsible by law for the financial performance of the nonprofit it governs. To fulfill this responsibility, board members must have access to the information they need to perform their critical fiduciary responsibilities. It is the chief executive's responsibility — with the help of senior management — to provide that financial information in clear and understandable form.

In both theory and practice, there are a number of distinctions between the roles of board members and senior executives:

KEY BOARD ROLES

- Legal responsibility as the organization's overseers.

- Governance, which includes

    - Establishing, with the chief executive, the mission and vision for the organization.

    - Setting direction and establishing specific goals — including financial components.

- Monitoring progress toward achieving the mission (actual outcomes compared to the established goals).

- Hiring and evaluating the chief executive (based on achievement or lack thereof).

KEY CHIEF EXECUTIVE ROLES

- Collaborating with the board to set the long-term mission.

- Managing the daily operations to help achieve the organizational mission.

- Providing information to the board that allows for a comprehensive understanding of whether goals are being met, including both financial and nonfinancial goals.

In concrete terms, the board is responsible for approving a long-term (five- to 10-year) financial plan and a short-term (one-year) capital and operating budget prepared by staff. Both of these major financial documents should ideally be the byproduct of the organization's strategic plan. In the interim, the board's oversight of management includes foremost the appropriate and timely review of the financial condition of the organization as presented in its financial statements. This requires that board members be knowledgeable and informed about the organization's financial status and underlying trends. The result of these efforts will be to help the chief executive and the senior staff decide how best to manage and optimize resources, especially in fiscally trying times.

TIPS FOR BOARD MEMBERS

1. Ensure the organization has a solid strategic plan. This will provide the executive staff with a road map for achieving agreed-upon goals.

2. Approve a financial plan that reflects the strategic plan. This allows the board to determine whether funding exists for its plans.

3. Ensure that the one-year operating and capital budgets constitute the key elements of the long-term strategic plan.

4. Help define specific metric indicators that relate to the organization's financial outcomes. This will be further discussed in Chapter 7.

2.

Types of Nonprofit Organizations

American companies can be organized as for-profit (investor-owned) or nonprofit. Both types of corporations may accrue a surplus of revenues in excess of expenses (which is called "profit" by a for-profit organization, and "net assets" by a nonprofit). However, in nonprofit organizations, expenditures, operating surpluses, and assets may not be used for the private benefit of any board members, officers, or employees.

Section 501(c) of the Internal Revenue Code (IRC) creates the federal definition of organizations that are generally exempt from income and most other federal taxes (state and local laws may further define and restrict which nonprofits are exempt from state and local taxes). The federal definition includes, among others, charities, social welfare organizations, and associations. If the proper filing requirements are met, the benefits of 501(c) status include

- Exemption from federal and state income taxes on any surplus of revenues over expenses.

- Exemption from federal and state taxes on capital gains from investments.

- Exemption from property taxes (in most states and localities).

- Exemption from state and local sales taxes (although they may have to be collected).

- The ability to obtain bond debt (to raise capital) where the interest income to the bond purchaser is generally tax exempt (thus allowing the debt to be issued at lower than commercial interest rates).

Section 501(c)(3) is the subsection under which most charities qualify for federal exemption. Those organizations must be operated exclusively for charitable, religious, educational, scientific, or other social welfare purposes. Additionally, charities must

- Be free of private inurement and private benefit.

- Have no *substantial* involvement in legislative activity.

- Have no participation in political or electioneering campaigns — except for education and get-out-the-vote purposes.

Designation as a 501(c)(3) nonprofit organization confers substantial financial benefits not available to for-profit organizations or other tax-exempt organizations. The most significant additional benefit is the ability to offer donors (individuals or for-profit corporations) a tax deduction for donations of cash or noncash assets.[1]

---

1. Even more important to some donors, there are cases where the tax deduction to a 501(c)(3) organization is valued at the stepped-up fair market (current) value of a donation. For example, stock that was purchased by a donor for $10,000 and that has increased in value to $100,000 by the time he donates it to a charity entitles the donor to a tax deduction for the current value of $100,000, not the original cost of only $10,000.

Thus, almost all charities find it extremely important to maintain their IRC Section 501(c)(3) status.

The IRC definition of charitable organizations is very broad and encompasses over a million different nonprofit organizations throughout the country. The major categories of charitable organizations are indicated in Box 1. Those nonprofit organizations represent many different types of services, different revenue streams (which may include various unrestricted and restricted donations), and different expenditure rationales (which may include various administrative overhead expenses as well as direct costs for carrying out programs).

Box 1

MAJOR CATEGORIES OF 501(C)(3) NONPROFIT ORGANIZATIONS

- Religious organizations
- Educational institutions
- Hospitals and other health care providers
- Libraries and research centers
- Community agencies
- Scientific research organizations
- Social service organizations
- Foundations

A key challenge to understanding financial statements is recognizing the wide diversity of nonprofit organizations and the multiplicity of audiences and clientele they serve. Because of this broad variety, no single financial statement example will appear typical. But throughout this book, we will utilize the financial statements of a fictional nonprofit organization that is meant to be an amalgamation of several types of nonprofit organizations operating throughout the country. While this fictional group may not be precisely like the nonprofit with which you are familiar, all the common and essential elements are shown to enable you to relate it to your organization.

TIPS FOR BOARD MEMBERS

1. Have an analysis prepared that quantifies the financial benefits of the organization's tax-exempt status. This allows the organization's board to understand the financial value of the status. And it provides additional talking points when discussing with outsiders the organization's value to the community.

2. In addition, analyze the value of the benefits being contributed to the community by your nonprofit organization at least once a year.

3.

Differentiating between Accounting and Finance Functions

At the outset, it is important to understand the differences between accounting functions and finance functions — and how board members relate to each.

ACCOUNTING FUNCTIONS

The accounting function enables a reader of financial statements to gain an understanding of the financial condition of the organization. There are five major elements to the accounting function, highlighted in Box 2. Each of the elements is crucial to the proper presentation of financial information. The first three elements are basic yet essential to the development and recording of the financial transactions of the organization. The last two elements, valuation and disclosure, set the accounting function apart from a purely bookkeeping task.

Box 2

ACCOUNTING FUNCTIONS

- Identifying and recording all valid transactions.

- Classifying financial transactions on a timely basis.

- Identifying the time period in which these transactions occurred (accrual accounting).

- Valuing these financial transactions in an appropriate manner.

- Disclosing these transactions in an adequate manner, in accordance with the organization's transparency practices.

Valuation — defined as assigning monetary worth to financial transactions — is the most crucial element among the accounting functions. Analysis of any statement of financial position (balance sheet) makes it quickly obvious that many of the line items are estimates and not actual financial values. These estimates are recorded in the form of allowances, accruals, adjustments, and reserves and are often given a value based on best judgment. Valuation, therefore, is part art as well as part science. Valuations take different forms depending on the type of account each may be and what *generally accepted accounting principles* (GAAP) dictates. For example, the valuation of cash is easy; investments are valued at the fair market value; inventory is valued at the lower of cost or fair market value; plant; property, and equipment are at historical cost while the related accumulated depreciation is an estimate of the useful life of the asset and the form of the GAAP depreciation employed. On the liability side of the balance sheet, every organization has a line item called "accrued liabilities." This line consists of estimated expenditures made throughout the organization before the month ended but no invoice has yet been received. It is the accountant's job, at the end of each month, to estimate, or value, the amount of dollars that need to be added to the balance sheet and statement of activities for these as yet unreceived invoices.

Disclosure, on the other hand, is a critical function because it requires that all transactions be produced and displayed in a relatively uniform manner. This uniformity is prescribed by the accounting industry through a basic set of understandings known as *generally accepted accounting principles* (GAAP). The Financial Accounting Standards Board (FASB), through periodic pronouncements called *statements*, enumerates and defines disclosure requirements for nonprofit organizations, and the American Institute of Certified Public Accountants (AICPA), in a periodically updated *Nonprofit Audit Guide*, sets down other important GAAP requirements for nonprofits to follow. These two sources provide the main guidance needed by the organization's accountants and auditors to develop and produce the most rational and understandable financial statements. In addition, one more authoritative accounting and auditing source that should be recognized is the *Government Auditing Standards*, first published in 1972, and commonly referred to as the "Yellow Book." These standards cover federal entities and those organizations receiving federal funds. Various laws require compliance with the comptroller general's auditing standards in connection with audits of federal entities and funds. Thus, these standards apply to any nonprofit organization that receives federal funds.

FINANCE FUNCTIONS

The accounting functions create standardized and understandable information that can be used for financial analysis. The finance function (see Box 3) provides the analysis that makes sense of the numbers generated by the accounting functions. Financial analysis goes beyond the numbers to ascertain trends and tendencies that may have positive or negative impacts on the organization. One widely used method for doing this is by developing ratios from the accounting numbers, which can provide the reader with enhanced information about the performance of the organization. Such ratios as operating margin percentage, the number of days cash on hand, and the debt service ratio can then be trended across time and compared to other organizations within the organization's sector (known as *benchmarking*). Conclusions can then be drawn from the analysis, courses of action evaluated, and decision made. (These concepts will be addressed in detail in Chapters 4 and 7.)

Conclusions drawn from ratio analysis have been the subject of some controversy in recent years. For example, boards sometimes try to set goals based on financial-ratio benchmarking, which management is then obligated to achieve. In many nonprofit agencies, these new goals — and accountability for achieving them — is a culture

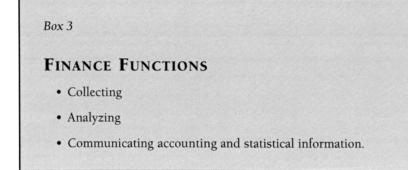

change, often challenged and sometimes unwelcomed. Occasionally, this resistance has led to outright deception: Joseph McCafferty reported in *CFO Magazine* in 2007 that at many organizations, some numbers (particularly fundraising expenses) reported on nonprofit financial statements (primarily the Statement of Financial Position and Statement of Activities) are being consistently misreported.[2] This is creating distorted efficiency and fundraising ratios. While we will review these later in Chapter 7, it is important now to note that it is the board's obligation to uncover any such misstatements and to ensure that the underlying accounting numbers are properly and accurately reported. Later chapters will highlight ways that boards can play their role in helping to ensure proper accounting and reporting.

TIPS FOR BOARD MEMBERS

1. Request from management and utilize financial ratios that will help in evaluating progress toward achieving the established goals of the organization.

2. Understand the information that lies behind each ratio that is used. For example, when examining the fundraising ratio, make sure that expenses for raising funds are honestly and fairly reported — and not omitted entirely. Since it is highly unlikely that a donation can be obtained without some outlay of expenses, if fundraising expenses are entirely absent or under-reported, the fundraising ratio will be distorted and deceptive. Ask questions of management and probe accounting and expense allocation practices.

3. Ensure that the organization presents its financial information according to GAAP.

---

2. "Misgivings — Recent Studies Raise an Uncharitable Question: Is Nonprofit Accounting Off Track," Joseph McCafferty, *CFO Magazine*, January 2007, page 38.

4.

Basic Elements of Audited Financial Statements

Since 1995, a generally accepted set of financial documents that provides basic financial information has been required for nonprofit organizations by Financial Accounting Standards Board Statement Number 117 (FAS 117). Review of these financial statements on a periodic basis by an organization's board is necessary for its required level of financial oversight:

- Statement of Financial Position (Balance Sheet)

- Statement of Activities (Income Statement)

- Statement of Cash Flows

- Statement of Functional Expenses (required for voluntary health and welfare organizations only; useful for all other nonprofit organizations)

- Notes (footnotes)

Creation of the statements above is the responsibility of management and they are typically produced monthly. The monthly statements are presented for the month just ended as well as for the year to date to provide valuable reference points and to allow the board to see how well the actual results follow projected assumptions. At year end, the year-to-date figures reflect the accumulation of the previous 12 months of transaction activities applied to the balance sheet and income statement. (FAS 117 also requires that the financial statements focus on the entity as a whole, rather than reporting on separate fund groups.)

Regardless of the line item, it is required that each entry be reported at *net realizable value*. This is defined as the amount in cash value that the organization expects either to receive or pay out. Net realizable values are almost always estimates and are developed utilizing generally accepted accounting principles (GAAP) methodologies. Each method has a considerable impact on the organization's bottom line and financial position; therefore, these elements must be fully understood by board members. The most significant methods, which decrease the value of the asset or the income, will be reviewed throughout this text.

OPINION LETTER

Before reviewing the actual financial statements, it should be noted that a complete set of audited financial statements will always include the auditor's *opinion letter*. The opinion letter has a basic structure set down in authoritative pronouncements by FASB and the AICPA. It is produced by the organization's external auditors at the conclusion of their review of the year-end figures, and it expresses judgment on whether the

Exhibit 1

AUDITOR'S OPINION LETTER

Little Four
Certified Public Accountants
123 Elm Street
Anytown, State 55555
732-555-1234
www.littlefour.biz

Board of Directors
ABC Charities, Inc.
987 Oak Road
Anytown, State 55555

We have audited the accompanying statement of financial position of ABC Charities, Inc. (a nonprofit organization) as of December 31, 2007 and 2006, and the related statement of activities, cash flows, and functional expenses for the year then ended. These financial statements are the responsibility of the Charities' management. Our responsibility is to express an opinion on the financial statements based on our audit.

We conducted our audit in accordance with auditing standards generally accepted in the United States of America. Those standards require that we plan and perform the audit to obtain reasonable assurance about whether the financial statements are free of material misstatement. An audit includes examining, on a test basis, evidence supporting the amounts and disclosures in the financial statements. An audit also includes assessing the accounting principles used and significant estimates made by management, as well as evaluating the overall financial statement presentation. We believe that our audit provides a reasonable basis for our opinion.

In our opinion, the accompanying financial statements present fairly, in all material respects, the financial position of ABC Charities, Inc. as of December 31, 2007 and 2006, and the changes in net assets and cash flows for the years then ended in conformity with accounting principles generally accepted in the United States of America.

Little Four, CPAs
March 4, 2008

management-prepared financial statements are "presented fairly" in conformance with GAAP and in accordance with generally accepted auditing standards.

Exhibit 1 illustrates a "clean" or "unqualified" opinion letter, the most prized auditor's judgment.[3] An opinion letter with three main paragraphs typically signifies a "clean" opinion. A fourth paragraph may also be added to include supplemental information. Additional paragraphs should be a red flag to board members because it often means the auditor believes that the statements are either not in compliance with GAAP (called a qualified or adverse opinion) or that the auditor is unable to form an opinion due to incomplete information (called a disclaimed opinion). Any qualified, disclaimed, or adverse opinion calls into question the integrity of the organization's financial procedures and position. Such opinions indicate serious problems and must be quickly and appropriately addressed by the board's audit and finance committee, as well as by the board as a whole.

STATEMENT OF FINANCIAL POSITION (BALANCE SHEET)

The *statement of financial position*, commonly known as the *balance sheet* (see Exhibit 2), has traditionally been recognized as the most important of all the financial statements due to the comprehensive and illuminating information contained in it. According to FAS 117, the balance sheet represents and is arranged to display the organization's financial assets, liabilities, and net assets (any accumulated financial surpluses since it came into existence). A nonprofit balance sheet is designed, through double-entry bookkeeping rules (an accounting technique that records every transaction as both a credit and a debit) to conform to the following equation: **Assets = Liabilities + Net Assets.**

At their simplest, *assets* are everything an organization **owns**, *liabilities* are everything an organization **owes**, and *net assets* are the difference between what an organization **owns** and what it **owes**. Thus, for example, cash and real property are assets, while accounts payable and bond debt are liabilities; the difference between the value of its assets and liabilities over the course of the organization's existence are the retained earnings, which are called net assets by nonprofit organizations.[4]

The balance sheet is the first and most important document that board members should know how to review and understand, particularly those line items that have the greatest impact on the organization's operations.[5] Depending on the specific type of services performed by the nonprofit organization, the crucial lines will likely be

---

3. If the nonprofit organization has expended more than $500,000 of federal awards in any one fiscal year, a "clean" opinion will look different than the one described in this paragraph.

4. On a for-profit company's balance sheet, net assets are called Shareholder or Owners Equity. Thus, in the for-profit (investor-owned) world, the balance sheet equation is **Assets = Liabilities + Owners Equity**. The major component of Owners Equity is "Paid-In Capital," which is the amount of cash paid to the company in return for ownership shares. Nonprofit balance sheets will never contain this line item because, by its very legal definition, there are no equity owners of a nonprofit and thus no person or company is ever legally permitted to pay in any capital in exchange for ownership rights.

5. While the numbers in themselves are significant, as will be shown later in this chapter and in Chapter 7, ratios developed based on these numbers are often even more revealing.

Exhibit 2

ABC Charities, Inc.
Statement of Financial Position (Balance Sheet)
At December 31, 2006 and 2007 (in thousands)

ASSETS:	December 2007	December 2006
Current Assets		
Cash	1,200	2,000
Investments — Short Term	6,500	5,400
Total Cash and Cash Equivalents	7,700	7,400
Gross Accounts Receivable	12,000	12,800
Less: Allowance for Doubtful Accounts	(2,800)	(2,600)
Net Patient Receivables	9,200	10,200
Unconditional Promises To Pay	5,000	5,000
Inventory	500	400
Prepaid Expenses	400	300
Other Current Assets	900	700
Total Current Assets	22,800	23,300
Long-Term Investments — Unrestricted	62,300	55,000
Trusteed Investments	10,000	12,200
Deferred Financing Costs	1,300	1,400
Other Noncurrent Assets	73,600	68,600
Property, Plant & Equipment		
Land and Land Improvements	2,000	2,000
Buildings	20,000	18,000
Leasehold Improvements	700	700
Equipment and Fixtures	10,500	9,000
Construction in Progress	1,500	1,000
Total PP&E	34,700	30,700
Less: Accumulated Depreciation	(18,000)	(15,000)
Net PP&E	16,700	15,700
TOTAL ASSETS	**113,100**	**107,600**

LIABILITIES:	December 2007	December 2006
Current Liabilities		
Accounts Payable	6,000	4,500
Current Retirement on L/T Debt	1,500	1,400
Total Current Liabilites	7,500	5,900
Long-Term Debt	64,800	66,200
Other Long-Term Liabilites	2,000	2,100
Total Long-Term Liabilites	66,800	68,300
TOTAL LIABILITES	74,300	74,200
NET ASSETS		
Unrestricted	32,600	27,900
Temporarily Restricted	4,200	4,200
Permanently Restricted	2,000	1,300
TOTAL NET ASSETS	38,800	33,400
TOTAL LIABILITIES AND NET ASSETS	113,100	107,600

- Assets

  - Cash

  - Accounts Receivable

  - Promises To Give (Pledges Receivable)

  - Property and Equipment (Fixed Assets)

- Liabilities

  - Accounts Payable

  - Accrued Liabilities

  - Current Portion of Long-Term Liabilities

  - Long-Term Liabilities (typically tax-exempt bonds)

- Net Assets

  - Unrestricted Net Asset Balances

  - Permanently Restricted Net Asset Balances

  - Temporarily Restricted Net Asset [Balances]

CASH

Cash is the first asset line on any balance sheet — and with good reason! Cash is the grease that lubricates the operation of any organization. Without a sufficient cash balance, an organization is unlikely to be able to meet its current liabilities (amounts owed for goods and services purchased and payroll obligations), as well as to pay back its longer-term liabilities such as tax-exempt bonds. An inadequate cash balance is an indication that the organization may be in decline, contracting, or even on the road to extinction.

On the balance sheet, cash is classified as either current or long-term. *Current cash* generally includes

- Checkbook cash (which is immediately available to pay bills).

- Cash equivalents (which are typically money market accounts, easily convertible to cash within one day).

- Certificates of deposit (if less than 365 days to maturity).

Noncurrent cash is generally classified as

- Cash designated for capital replacement and acquisition that is invested in longer-term assets (such as Treasury bills or bonds).

- Trustees' investments (such as board-designated reserves and cash set aside from bond proceeds to be used in capital projects).

Determining whether the levels of short-term and long-term (noncurrent) cash are sufficient is critical to an understanding of the organization's financial health. Management should be expected to present information on a monthly basis in a trended format (preferably as a graph) to highlight the movement of the organization's cash balances.

ACCOUNTS RECEIVABLE

Many nonprofit organizations are service organizations, such as universities, hospitals, and social service agencies. Organizations that charge fees for their services usually provide those services before payments are made; the money owed by the client or patient or student for the services rendered are known as *accounts receivable*. In some nonprofit organizations, the accounts receivable may be the largest current asset.

The accounting transaction creates a receivable (a debit) on the balance sheet and a credit to service revenues on the income statement. So, for example, a transaction to record the tuition money due from student Joe Smith would be entered on a university's balance sheet accordingly:

Debit: Accounts Receivable (recorded on the balance sheet)	$15,000
Credit: Service Revenue (e.g., tuition) (recorded on the income statement)	$15,000

Converting accounts receivable assets into cash is a major goal of nonprofit organizations with substantial accounts receivables. The preferred way to move receivables to zero is through cash collections (at a rate of 100 percent of the receivable). A less-favored method is through write-downs and write-offs, which reduce the anticipated cash due by converting receivables to bad debts. However, the consequence of write-offs and write-downs is a reduction of revenues on the income statement. So, for instance, a transaction to reflect the fact that student Joe Smith can only pay $12,000 of his tuition instead of the full $15,000 would be expressed as a reduction to previously recorded service revenue:

Debit: Cash (balance sheet)	$12,000
Debit: Service Revenue Adjustment — Uncollectible (income statement)	$3,000
Credit: Accounts Receivable — Joe Smith (balance sheet)	$15,000

The above transaction is a direct write-off for bad debts (uncollectible accounts). The more common method for recording bad-debt expenses and write-offs of customer accounts is through the use of an allowance (or reserve) for accounts that are doubtful of collection. This additional account incorporates a monthly estimate of the value of write-offs that are expected against the current accounts receivable balances, based upon the length of time that the accounts have remained unpaid or overdue and on the historic trends for such accounts. Typically, the difference between this month's allowance for doubtful accounts and last month's allowance for such accounts becomes this month's bad-debt expense, shown as an operating expense on the income statement:

This month's allowance for doubtful accounts	$5,000
Last month's allowance for doubtful accounts	$4,800
Bad debt expense — current month	$200

Because they reduce revenues on the income statement, bad debts and write-offs should generally be discouraged as the method for reducing the level of accounts receivable. The board of directors and senior management should be in accord when emphasizing to the organization's finance division the need to maximize cash collections and to minimize bad debts and write-offs.

PROMISES TO GIVE (PLEDGES RECEIVABLE)

In many nonprofit organizations, *unconditional promises to give* (previously known as pledges receivable) may represent a significant component of total assets. This is the case when the organization's primary revenue stream is from contributions. When contributions are promised or pledged (but not yet received), the organization posts contribution revenue to its statement of activities and a similar amount to the unconditional-promise-to-give line item on the balance sheet.

A question that generally arises regarding promises to give is "when is a pledge really a pledge?" According to Statement of Financial Accounting Standards 116 (FAS 116) paragraph 6, "a promise to give is a written or oral agreement to contribute cash or other assets to another entity; however, to be recognized in financial statements there must be sufficient evidence in the form of verifiable documentation that a promise was made and received. A communication that does not indicate clearly whether it is a promise is considered an unconditional promise to give if it indicates an unconditional intention to give that is legally enforceable." Thus it is incumbent on the nonprofit organization to have pledge policies in place that are (1) in line with the FAS 116 standards and (2) effective in minimizing the risk of noncollection of pledges, whether made through the mail or by phone.

The unconditional-promises-to-give balance sheet line is reported as a net number, already reflecting any reduction for the estimated amount of promises that will be uncollectible. The amount of the uncollectible is calculated based on historical averages and the amount of time that a pledge has remained unpaid. (It is the equivalent to the allowance for doubtful accounts applied to accounts receivable.)

As with any receivable, it is in the interest of the organization to minimize the net amount on this line at any point in time. Good management mandates that these promises be monitored and reasonable efforts made to collect the promises to give.

PROPERTY AND EQUIPMENT (FIXED ASSETS)

Many nonprofit organizations, particularly those that provide services, often have a substantial percentage of their assets in so-called *fixed assets*. Fixed assets are tangible items, such as land, land improvements, buildings, building equipment, movable equipment, furniture, leasehold improvements, or capitalized leases. Organizations are permitted to develop their own reasonable policies for the capitalization of fixed assets, based on the useful life of the asset. For example, many organizations classify a fixed asset as any tangible item that has a useful life greater than one year and a minimum purchase price of $500. Other organizations may choose a higher minimum purchase price or a longer life span. The longer the life and the lower the minimum purchase price, the more assets will be reflected in this line item (and the larger the *plant ledger*).[6] Generally, each organization is permitted to develop its own policy (known as the capitalization policy) for classifying items it owns as fixed assets, based on reasonable criteria or standard industry practices.

The plant ledger and the balance sheet reflect the current value of a fixed asset, which is determined by subtracting the depreciation expense over an asset's life (to date) from its original cost. This is known as *accumulated depreciation*. On the balance sheet, the gross property and equipment totals, less their accumulated depreciation, equals the net property and equipment line. This is also commonly referred to as the *net book value*.

Depreciation is, of course, a key concept on the balance sheet. The depreciation expense concept allows an organization to take each fixed asset on the plant ledger (a building or piece of equipment costing more than the minimum price chosen as part of the organization's capitalization policy) and to depreciate (or amortize) it over the useful life of the fixed asset. In addition to being a major element of the accumulated depreciation line, depreciation is also considered a noncash expense, not a fixed asset, and is an important line item on the Statement of Activities. As an example, if an organization paid $1,000,000 for its office building, and determined that the useful life of the building was 25 years, the annual depreciation expense to be recorded in the Statement of Activities, according to GAAP, would be $40,000 ($1,000,000 divided by 25 years). The other side of this accounting entry would be $40,000 added to the accumulated depreciation.

ACCOUNTS PAYABLE AND ACCRUED LIABILITIES

Accounts payable represents the amount of money known to be owed to trade vendors (i.e., companies that supply the organization with goods and services) and *accrued liabilities* is the amount estimated to be owed to vendors and suppliers (accrued expenses) that have provided goods or services to the organization. Accrued liabilities may also include vacation accruals, accrued payroll, and accrued pension.

Accounts payables include all unpaid invoices that have been recorded, while accrued expenses are estimates of the costs for services that have been performed, but for which invoices have not been sent by the vendor. Both major items become liabilities for which cash will need to be paid out in the near future.

Accrual of payables and liabilities is one of the five major accounting functions (see Chapter 3). It is employed to match the time period in which expenses are incurred

---

6. The plant ledger is a subsidiary ledger of the general ledger, where all the elements for each individual asset are recorded. The key elements are the asset's description, original cost, date of acquisition, annual depreciation expense, and accumulated depreciation.

with the concurrent revenues produced. Accrual accounting is generally required by GAAP because it shows a more reasonable expression of the true state of an organization's financial position than does the *cash method* of accounting. The cash method — which does not necessarily record the obligation of the organization to pay for services or goods that were required to produce the cash receipts or does not do so in the same time period — can be very misleading to the reader of a nonprofit's financial statements. For this reason, most nonprofit organizations currently use the accrual method for their accounting.

CURRENT PORTION OF LONG-TERM LIABILITIES

The current principal of outstanding bonds due to be paid by the organization within the next 12 months is referred to as the *current portion of long-term liabilities*. These payments may be due and payable quarterly, semiannually, or annually, based on the terms of the bonds and the amortization schedule. After the original bond issuance is recorded (see Long-Term Liabilities below), the current portion is reserved and reported separately on the balance sheet in the current liabilities section. The example below reclassifies the current portion of the principal on the bonds payable from the long-term section to the current-liability section.

Debit: Bonds Payable — Long Term (balance sheet)	$400,000
Credit: Bonds Payable — Current Portion (balance sheet)	$400,000

LONG-TERM LIABILITIES

In larger nonprofit organizations, the most common type of long-term liability is tax-exempt bonds payable. In smaller nonprofit organizations, a common type of long-term liability is mortgages or notes payable. In both cases, this line represents the amount of cash that the organization has received (less discounts and other fees) through the issuance of debt. These proceeds are typically used to finance a major capital purchase, expansion, or renovation that will improve the operations and services of the organization. In the case of a bond offering, the accounting treatment for this type of transaction records the cash received and the liabilities created by the issuance of bonds for expansion purposes, as in this example:

Debit: Cash (balance sheet)	$9,500,000
Debit: Deferred Financing Costs (balance sheet)	$500,000
Credit: Bonds Payable (balance sheet)	$10,000,000

The deferred financing costs are amortized (allocated) over the life of the bond, which could range from 10 to 30 years. When the deferred costs are reduced on a monthly basis, they become an income statement expense, thus decreasing the operating and net margins. The transaction below represents the write-off of the deferred financing costs on the balance sheet on a monthly basis over a 30-year period.

> Debit: Bond Amortization Cost $1,389
> (income statement) (*$500,000 divided by 360 monthly periods*
> *(may be combined with depreciation)* [*30 years x 12 months per year*])
> Credit: Deferred Financing Costs (balance sheet) $1,389

Mortgage receipts will have similar balance sheet treatment.

UNRESTRICTED NET ASSET BALANCES

Unrestricted net assets are the accumulation of all the organization's financial surpluses since it came into existence. (It is the equivalent of retained earnings on a for-profit balance sheet.) The unrestricted net asset balance assists board members in determining the underlying financial worth of the organization, because it is the value left after the organization's total liabilities are subtracted from its total assets. Boards need to be aware that these balances may not be available for future expansion or use during adverse times. These balances do not necessarily represent available cash or other liquid assets but could be related to property. It is always judicious to monitor trends of an organization's unrestricted net assets over time; most boards expect to see a continuously rising trend for this balance sheet line, as it likely represents consistently positive operating margins.

RESTRICTED NET ASSET BALANCES

These are a nonprofit's assets (usually cash) that a donor has restricted in their use. The restrictions are usually in the form of either a time limit for use or a restriction on what the asset may be used for. FAS 117 requires that restricted net assets on nonprofit balance sheets be divided into two major categories: permanently restricted and temporarily restricted. The differences can be summarized as follows.

Temporarily Restricted Net Assets

The use of the asset is restricted by a donor, but the restriction(s) can usually be met either with the passage of time or by the purpose being fulfilled. The simplest example of such a restricted asset is a one-year grant from a foundation to a nonprofit for a specific work plan. To meet the restrictions, the nonprofit must fulfill the work plan within the year's time limit. But restrictions can also be more complicated: For example, a donor may stipulate that the principal of his $1,000,000 donation cannot be utilized for the first 20 years; only the interest may be used by the nonprofit. However, at the end of the 20 years, the donor specifies that the principal will no longer be restricted. Therefore, the $1,000,000 is classified as a temporarily restricted net asset for 20 years, at which point, the nonprofit may reclassify it as unrestricted, if it so chooses.

It is the responsibility of management — by careful tracking of expenditures — to demonstrate to the auditors each year whether the use restrictions of a restricted asset have been fulfilled, so that the auditors may then certify that the asset (usually cash) has been used as the donor intended.

Permanently Restricted Net Assets

The use of the asset is restricted by a donor, and the restriction never expires, nor can it be removed. An example of a permanently restricted net asset is a donation to endow a university faculty position. Such endowments often stipulate that the original donated principal can never be reduced or used, and that only the interest earned on the principal may be used to fund the position in perpetuity.

STATEMENT OF ACTIVITIES (INCOME STATEMENT)

The statement of activities, also known as the *income statement*, is a compilation of all revenues and expenses of a nonprofit organization. The statement also shows the excess or deficit of revenues over expenses (sometimes referred to as the *operating margin*) and the *change in net assets* (also referred to as the net margin). See Exhibit 3.

GAAP requires that revenues and expenditures be classified and shown as unrestricted, temporarily restricted, or permanently restricted. Further, GAAP requires that expenses be categorized into program services, management, and fundraising expenses. (It also requires that expenses be reported on a functional basis, which will be reviewed later in the *statement of functional expenses*.) There are several important concepts in the statement of activities that board members should be aware of.

Exhibit 3

ABC Charities, Inc.
Statement of Activites
For the Year-to-Date Ending
December 31, 2006 and 2007
(in thousands)

PUBLIC SUPPORT AND REVENUES:
  Net Service Revenues
  Contributions
  Grants
Total Suport and Revenue

EXPENSES:
Program Services
Management and General
Fundraising
Total Expenses

Excess of Support and Revenue over Expenses

NON-OPERATING INCOME (EXPENSES):
  Gain/(Loss) on investments
Total Non-Operating Income

Excess of Support and Total Revenue over Expenses (Total margin)

  Net Assets, Beginning of Year
Change in net unrealized gains
  and losses on investments

Net Assets, End of Year

| | Twelve months ended 12/31/07 | | | | |
Unrestricted	Temporarily Restricted	Permanently Restricted	Total 2007	Total 2006	Percentage Change
43,600	10,000	-	53,600	50,000	7.20%
9,000	-	700	9,700	9,000	7.78%
3,400	-	-	3,400	3,200	6.25%
56,000	10,000	700	66,700	62,200	7.23%
40,600	7,000	-	47,600	45,800	3.30%
10,190	3,000	-	13,190	12,000	12.33%
710	-	-	710	700	1.43%
51,500	10,000	0	61,500	58,500	5.13%
4,500	0	700	5,200	3,700	40.54%
1,200	-	-	1,200	1,000	20.00%
1,200	-	-	1,200	1,000	20.00%
5,700	-	700	6,400	4,700	36.17%
59,500	4,200	1,300	65,000	62,300	4.33%
(1,000)	-	-	(1,000)	(2,000)	-50.00%
64,200	4,200	2,000	70,400	65,000	8.31%

SUPPORT AND REVENUE

Service Revenues

One of the most common sources of revenue for nonprofits is fee-based services to clients, patients, or students. Those revenues must be recorded for the services provided and reported on the statement of activities at their *net realizable value*. Thus, if discounts are provided for various clients, then the discounts must be applied against all the gross revenue being recorded. (This is a major tenet of GAAP.) If the discounts are not appropriately applied, the revenues on the statement of activities will be overstated and misleading to readers, including the board.

Depending on the sector in which a nonprofit operates, the recording (posting) of revenues should be in conformance with GAAP within that sector. For example, colleges will record their revenues based on the general accepted methods within university accounting rules, while hospitals will record their revenue based on the generally accepted methods within the health care industry.

Contributions

Because contributions make up a major portion of the revenues of so many public charities, it is important for those boards to understand the rules governing the recognition of contribution revenue. These contributions can be in the form of cash, stock, bonds, art, property, or any other tangible asset that has value.

Contributions to 501(c)(3) groups are encouraged by tax laws that permit individual (not corporate) tax-paying donors to deduct the current fair market value of their contributions on their tax returns. (While the current value of cash is always known, donated assets other than cash may not be so easy to value.) There are multiples rules set down by the IRS regarding the valuation by the contributors of donations other than cash. It is the responsibility of the donor to determine the value, not the nonprofit organization. Contributors can find the rules at IRS Publication 526 — Charitable Contributions and IRS Publication 561 — Determining the Value of Donated Property. FAS 116 specifies the definition and accounting treatment of contributions by nonprofits:

- A contribution is defined as being an unconditional, nonreciprocal transfer of assets to a nonprofit. "Unconditional" means that a contribution with a donor-imposed condition, such as a matching requirement, should not be recognized (i.e., recorded in the financial statements) until the condition has been met. "Nonreciprocal" means that the donor does not receive anything of value in return for the contribution. It should be noted that the issue of a conditional versus an unconditional contribution is very important and is an area that has been known to cause great concern for board members and their management. The first decision when a gift or award is received is to decide whether the condition placed on it can be met. If there is a risk and/or it is dependent on some outside forces not controlled by the nonprofit organization, then it should not be recorded as revenue. So if a condition for a $100,000 gift is that it has to be matched by 100 percent board participation of gifts totaling $100,000, some thought must be given before simply recording it as revenue. If this particular board has never had more than 20 percent of its members give and never raised more $7,000 among them, then the revenue should not be recorded. However, if the board is very influential and continually has had 100 percent participation with consistently more than $100,000 raised, then the revenue should be recognized at the time of the gift. Once it is determined that the award is not "conditional" and can be recorded when notice of the award is received, then the next decision is the asset class — is it unrestricted, temporarily restricted, or permanently restricted?

- A contribution is recorded, not just when cash is received, but also if and when a pledge is made. This means the recipient organization must record a pledge receivable and contribution income prior to actually receiving the cash.

- A contribution is recorded immediately as income, even though it may have donor restrictions that have not been met. This is based on FASB's determination that a restricted contribution only limits the use of the funds, but does not result in a liability for the nonprofit. Therefore, a contribution is recognized as income even though the related expenditure to satisfy a restriction may not be made until a future period.

Grants

Another significant benefit of 501(c)(3) tax-exempt designation for nonprofits is the ability to accept grants from charitable and corporate foundations and from government agencies. Grants can be restricted or unrestricted and are recorded at their fair market value when received.

Grants are typically made to a nonprofit organization by corporations, foundations, and government agencies to help the nonprofit meet its charitable mission. Grant revenue is a major source of funding for many nonprofits and is often used to augment donations and service revenues, enabling an organization to expand the services and support needed by its clients, patients, or students.

Expenses

FAS 117 requires that expenses must be categorized and grouped into program services, management, and fundraising functions. While practices vary widely from organization to organization in the nonprofit sector as to how expenses are categorized, it is important to understand the basic guidelines. The three major categories prescribed by FAS 117 are

1. *Program Services*: These are the expenditures, goods, and services used in activities to fulfill the purpose or mission of the organization. In general, the most common expenses include salaries and benefits for staff, supplies, purchased services, and even the depreciation allocated for the buildings and equipment used to service the organization's clientele.

2. *Management and General*: This category includes expenditures on general oversight and management (except for direct conduct of program services or

fundraising activities), general record keeping, budgeting, finance, and other general and administrative activities. Also included are expenses that are categorized as indirect, shared, or overhead — those that are essential to program administration but are difficult to allocate to specific programs. A few examples of overhead expenses include allocated portions of a chief executive's time or lease costs for shared space (such as restrooms). It is important for boards to recognize the indispensable value of these supporting services to the function and success of the organization's program services.

3. *Fundraising*: This category recognizes expenses incurred in the solicitation of contributions and grants from individuals, foundations, government agencies, and others. It can include costs of fundraising activities as widely varied as direct mail, a walk-a-thon, or a fundraising dinner. What is important for board members is to recognize that this is where all the expenses incurred in the production of fundraising revenues is captured. It is essential to some important ratios and is useful to the board, particularly for planning and monitoring.

Because it is required that each organization assign expenses among these functions according to generally accepted accounting principles and practices within its sector, board members may want to do additional reading on the subject or initiate discussion with the group's external auditors.

Non-Operating Revenues and Expenses

An organization may also have revenues and expenses that are not related to its programs or mission. These are called *non-operating revenues and expenses*. The most common item that falls into this category is realized investment income or losses — gain or loss from the sale of invested assets (such as common stock or mutual funds) that are owned by the organization. There are very specific accounting rules for reporting these revenues. (Note: *unrealized* investment income or losses are not shown in this section of the statement, but rather as a Change in Net Assets.)

Change in Net Assets

As stated in the previous section, *unrealized income or losses on investments* (increases or decreases to the value of the investment instruments, such as stocks and bonds) are reported as a change in net assets. The unrealized income or losses on investments are the differences between the *fair market values* of all the organization's assets that have potential for investment and that are still being held by the organization. The change is shown as of the end of the last accounting period and for the current accounting period.

FAS 124 requires that unrealized income or losses be reported on the statement of activities after the "total margin" line because they are *unrealized* and therefore only have the potential to influence the bottom line of the organization. Therefore, the FASB requires that they be shown, but after actual operating revenues and expenses. See the next to last line in Exhibit 3 (page 22).

STATEMENT OF CASH FLOWS

The *statement of cash flows* (see Exhibit 4) is also mandated by FAS 117. It reports the sources and uses of the organization's short-term cash and cash equivalents for the period concurrent with the statement of activities (income statement). It is a summary of where the organization's cash came from and how it was used.

The statement of cash flows is often overlooked as a source of information for board members and administrators, but it is necessary to complete the reader's understanding of a nonprofit organization's financial condition. The most important line items to review are net investments, capital expenditures, proceeds from the issuance of long-term debt, and payments on long-term debt.

NET INVESTMENTS

If an organization chooses to use any of its short-term cash to invest in higher yielding, longer-term financial instruments (e.g., bonds or mutual funds), the total net value of the investments is reported on this line of the statement of cash flows. It is important for board members to review this line if there was a reduction of short-term cash to which this could have been a contributing factor.

CAPITAL EXPENDITURES — NET

As one of the most important lines on the statement of cash flows, *capital expenditures — net* is the only place in the entire set of financial statements where a reader can determine the total net amount of cash spent on fixed assets. A board member should review the amount reported on this line and compare it to the depreciation expense reported above it on the statement.[7]

If the net capital expenditures plus payments on long-term debt (see page 29) exceed the reported depreciation expense, then the organization has spent more cash on new fixed assets and old debt principal than it recorded as operating expenses. This will typically translate as net cash outlays for the organization. It is an area that may need to be reviewed by management and the board if the organization is experiencing cash flow shortages.

PROCEEDS FROM THE ISSUANCE OF LONG-TERM DEBT

When a nonprofit organization needs to spend money to expand its operations (renovations, new facilities, new equipment), it has several options. It can use accumulated cash or investments, create more cash through increased giving, such as a capital campaign, lease (if appropriate), or borrow money. If the amount needed is large and borrowing appears to be the best option, an organization may turn to tax-exempt bonds as its means of debt financing. Tax-exempt financing will have a lower

---

7. Depreciation is an expense reported on the statement of activities (income statement), but it is also a noncash expense, which is why it is added back on the cash flow statement.

Exhibit 4

ABC Charities, Inc.
Statement of Cash Flows
For the Year-to-Date Ended December 31, 2006 and 2007

	2007	2006
Cash Flows from Operating Activites:		
Increase (Decrease) in net assets	6,400	4,700
Change in net unrealized gains and losses	(1,000)	(2,000)
on investments other than trading securities		
Increase (Decrease) in cash flows from operating activities:		
Depreciation and Amortization	3,100	2,900
Net Accounts Receivable (increase) decrease	1,000	(700)
Other Current Assets (increase) decrease	(200)	1,400
A/P & Accrued Liabilites (decrease) increase	1,500	200
Other Long-Term Liabilites (decrease) increase	(100)	1,000
Current Portion of Long-Term Debt (decrease)	100	100
Net cash provided by (used in) operating activities	10,800	7,600
Cash Flows from Investing Activities (increase) decrease:		
Net Investments	(5,100)	0
Other Noncurrent Assets	0	(200)
Capital Expenditures — Net	(4,000)	(3,500)
Net cash provided by (used in) investing activities	(9,100)	(3,700)
Cash Flows from Financing Activities:		
Proceeds from the Issuance of Long-Term Debt	0	0
Payments on Long-Term Debt	(1,400)	(1,300)
Net cash provided by (used in) financing activities	(1,400)	(1,300)
Net Increase (Decrease) in Cash and Cash Equivalents	300	2,600
Cash and Cash Equivalents, beginning of year	7,400	4,800
Cash and Cash Equivalents, end of year	7,700	7,400

interest rate cost than taxable financing (as from a bank), and, since it is legally available to 501(c)(3) nonprofit organizations, it is a preferred option, because it will generally be the lowest-cost borrowing option. The proceeds from the issuance of new long-term bond debt will be reported on the cash flow statement. It indicates to the reader that the reason for the increase in cash is due to the proceeds from the bond issuance.

PAYMENTS ON LONG-TERM DEBT

Whenever an organization borrows long-term debt money, it is, of course, obliged to pay it back. In traditional bond offerings, the payment of interest to borrowers is customarily made every six months, while the principal payments are made once a year. While interest expenses are accounted for within the statement of activities as a cash item, the principal payback is not recorded as an expense. Therefore, the reduction for the cash paid to borrowers is seen most clearly on the statement of cash flows.

The board has fiduciary responsibilities in relation to bond or other borrowings: First, it needs to ensure that the organization will have the cash available to meet its debt obligations, including the principal payments as well as the interest. The most common sources for making these paybacks would be

- Positive cash flows based on positive net margins, and/or

- Utilization of depreciation expenses already factored into the net margin calculation.[8]

Second, if a nonprofit organization has outstanding bonds on the open market, they are likely subject to bond covenants. These agreements may require the organization to meet certain financial ratios at the time of filing the required quarterly and/or annual financial reports. It is incumbent on the board to make certain that these covenants are reviewed, and to ensure that all pledges made therein are met by management. Penalties for noncompliance, detailed in the original bond document, can be severe: The harshest allows the bond holders to demand immediate payback of the bond funds — which is certainly not a desired outcome. The board should require management to present a bond covenant analysis quarterly and/or annually. The analysis should include trends across time (in graph form).

STATEMENT OF FUNCTIONAL EXPENSES

While FAS 117 requires that only voluntary health and welfare nonprofit organizations report expenditures by functional expenses (see Exhibit 5), nevertheless, many other nonprofit organizations have begun including this

---

8. If the organization accesses long-term debt funding through a traditional mortgage rather than a bond, it will have a level debt service payment stream (the total payment is the same each month, but as each month passes the principal payment increases and the interest expense payment decreases), but the two main sources of payback will still apply.

report, since, in the words of FAS 117, it "helps donors, creditors, and others in assessing an organization's service efforts, including the costs of its services and how it uses resources."

The *statement of functional expenses* enables a reader to determine quickly if an organization is utilizing its revenue and support dollars primarily to achieve its program mission, or using them largely to pay for support services, such as fundraising or administrative activities. It is useful for board members to compare the percentages spent on each category of functional expenses by their organization to the percentages spent by other, similar groups. Many nonprofit sectors, such as arts groups, libraries, hospitals, and others, have developed their own benchmarks for the percentage of expenses that are usually and customarily devoted to program services versus supporting services.

The primary functional classifications and their definitions (discussed in detail earlier under the Statement of Activities on page 22) are

Exhibit 5

Statement of Functional Expenses
ABC Charities, Inc.
For the Year-to-Date Ended December 31, 2006 and 2007

	Mental Health	Substance Abuse	Clinic
STAFFING EXPENSES			
Salaries	8,000	6,000	11,000
Fringe Benefits	1,680	1,260	2,310
Contract Services	720	540	990
Total Salaries and Benefits	10,400	7,800	14,300
NONSTAFFING EXPENSES			
Medical Supplies	1,000	400	1,600
Office Supplies	400	200	380
Other Expenses	800	500	800
Rent Expense	500	720	1,400
Legal	-	-	
Accounting	-	-	
Bad Debt Expense	500	200	700
Depreciation — Buildings and Equipment	600	200	1,600
Interest & Financing Expenses	600	200	1,800
Total Nonstaffing Expenses	4,400	2,420	8,280
TOTAL EXPENSES	14,800	10,220	22,580

- *Program services*: expenditures, goods, and services used in activities to fulfill the purpose or mission of the organization.

- *Supporting activities*:

  - *Management and general*: expenditures on general oversight, administrative, and management functions.

  - *Fundraising*: expenses incurred in the solicitation of contributions from individuals, foundations, government agencies, and others.

  - *Membership development*: costs of soliciting for prospective members and membership dues, membership relations, and similar activities.

The allocation of so-called joint, shared, or overhead expenses between program services and supporting activities is a point of controversy for many groups and nonprofit sectors. While GAAP tries to define the parameters within which certain expenses like space costs, management costs, and fundraising costs are allocated

Program Support	Total and General	Management Fund-Raising	Total Expenses	2007 Total Expenses	2006 % Change
25,000	9,000	400	34,400	33,000	4.24%
5,250	1,890	85	7,225	6,930	4.26%
2,250	-	-	2,250	2,500	-10.00%
32,500	10,890	485	43,875	42,430	3.41%
3,000	-	-	3,000	2,820	6.38%
980	200	50	1,230	1,200	2.50%
2,100	500	50	2,650	1,970	34.52%
2,620	-	25	2,645	2,500	5.80%
-	300	-	300	280	7.14%
-	100	-	100	100	0.00%
1,400	-	100	1,500	1,000	50.00%
2,400	600	-	3,000	2,900	3.45%
2,600	600	-	3,200	3,300	-3.03%
15,100	2,300	225	17,625	16,070	9.68%
47,600	13,190	710	61,500	58,500	5.13%

between the two, the application of such guidelines may be — and often is — inconsistent.

For example, the AICPA (in Statement of Position 98-2) outlines the criteria for allocation of certain "joint" costs between program and fundraising, but the application of those criteria may vary dramatically from organization to organization. The result can be, for example, that one group may allocate a much greater percentage of direct mail costs to public education (a program service) and a much smaller percentage to fundraising (a supporting activity) than another organization with similar direct mail activities, resulting in dramatically different ratios of program to supporting services for the two groups.

Likewise, time spent by an organization's chief executive on program activities may rightfully be allocated to that, rather than to administrative, supporting costs. Similarly, various shared expenses, such as rent, utilities, insurance, and other items may be divided by one organization by a reasonable, consistent allocation methodology. But a different methodology used by another group to allocate those same costs — while also reasonable and consistent — may produce widely varying results from the former.

Any internal allocation guidelines that are reasonable, justifiable, and consistent, are likely to be accepted by auditors and donors. But this lack of standard allocation practices makes functional accounting less than reliable as a benchmark standard.

FOOTNOTES

No set of financial statements is complete without the *footnotes* or *notes* that provide further crucial information to the reader about the organization's financial policies and procedures. Many footnotes are required by GAAP and, in some cases, even the format is prescribed. For example, the first footnote on all financial statements is a summary of significant accounting policies; it discloses the various accounting policies and practices used by the organization in the creation of its accounting books and records (see Exhibit 6 on page 34).

Additional notes may be used to describe, in detail, the nonprofit's programs, investments and investment policies, affiliated organization investments, property and equipment, lease commitments, contingent liabilities, long-term debts and leases, joint cost allocations, related party transactions, pension plans, temporarily and permanently restricted assets, and any significant subsequent events.

Board members overlook the notes at their peril, for they provide essential additional information about key issues that affect an organization's financial status — and they are necessary to a full understanding of the financial statements.

THE SARBANES-OXLEY (SOX) ACT AND ITS RELEVANCE TO NONPROFIT ORGANIZATIONS

The Sarbanes-Oxley Act set new standards for investor-owned companies in 2002. The law came about because highly publicized accounting improprieties at investor-owned companies, such as Enron, Worldcom, and Xerox, provoked such a public outcry that Congress was prompted to legislate better accounting controls for investor-owned companies. It was enacted to ensure that internal controls over financial reporting became one of management's highest priorities by codifying board, governance, management, and auditor responsibility for maintaining board objectivity and auditor independence and by ensuring that companies have processes and controls in place to produce timely and accurate financial reports for boards and shareholders.

SOX's main provisions:

- Require establishment of an independent and competent audit committee of the board;

- Require periodic change of auditors, prohibit auditing firms from providing non-audit services concurrent with auditing services, and increase disclosure of all critical accounting policies and practices by the auditors;

- Impose disclosure and conflict-of-interest requirements on boards of directors;

- Require public disclosure of internal control mechanisms, material off-balance sheet adjustments, and corrections to past financial statements; and

- Provide protections for whistleblowers and prohibit retaliation against them.

But, with two exceptions, the SOX legislation applies only to publicly traded companies. So why discuss these provisions in a book devoted to nonprofits?

First, the goal of SOX is certainly relevant and appropriate for any nonprofit organization. The primary aim of SOX is to ensure that the financial information being reported to a board by management is accurate and can be relied upon in its decision making. SOX provides corporate directors with added assurance that auditors are independent and that internal controls are adequate — without which there is no reasonable expectation that the numbers being reported have authenticity.

Second, the nonprofit sector has had its share of similar scandals. This has prompted several watchdog organizations, legislators, and standard-setting groups for several segments within the nonprofit community to study SOX-like controls in more detail. For example, in the health care industry, the National Association of Insurance Commissioners has adopted revisions to its Model Audit Rule that would impose SOX-like requirements in three areas: management reports on Internal Control of Financial Reporting, the audit committee's composition and responsibilities, and auditor independence and scope of services. In California, the first state to adopt such a law, the Nonprofit Integrity Act of 2004 requires that any charity registered with the attorney general and receiving annual gross revenues of $2 million or more must form an audit committee.[9]

Studies of investor-owned companies have shown that stronger internal controls have resulted in increased investor confidence and long-term shareholder value — which

---

9. The Sarbanes-Oxley Act and Implications for Nonprofit Organizations, Boardsource, 2006, http://www.boardsource.org/dl.asp?document_id=558.

Exhibit 6

ABC Charities, Inc.
Notes to Financial Statements
Years Ended December 31, 2007 and 2006

1. SUMMARY OF SIGNIFICANT POLICIES

    a. Operations

    ABC Charities, Inc. is a not-for-profit health services organization, providing general and mental health and substance abuse services.

    The Charities is exempt from federal income taxes under Section 501(c)(3) of the Internal Revenue Code and from Federal Unemployment Compensation tax.

    Contributions to the Charities are deductible for income tax purposes within the limitations of the law.

    b. Basis of Accounting

    The accompanying financial statements have been prepared on the accrual basis of accounting and are presented in accordance with Financial Accounting Standards Board Statements No. 117, Financial Statements of Not-for-Profit Organizations. Under SFAS 117, the Charities is required to report information regarding its financial position and activities according to three classes of net assets: unrestricted net assets, temporarily restricted net assets, and permanently restricted net assets. The Charities had unrestricted and temporarily restricted net assets in 2007 and 2006.

    c. Net Assets Accounting

    ABC Charities reports grants and gifts as restricted support if they are received with donor stipulations that limit the use of donated assets. When a donor restriction expires, that is, when a stipulated time restriction ends or purpose restriction is accomplished, temporarily restricted net assets are reclassified to unrestricted net assets and reported in the statement of activities as net assets released from restrictions. Grants and donations of fixed assets are recorded as unrestricted support, unless explicit donor stipulations specify how those assets must be used.

    d. Property and Equipment

    Property and equipment are stated at cost or, if donated, at the approximate fair market value at the date of donation.

    Depreciation is computed using the straight-line method over the estimated useful lives of related assets, which range as follows:

Land Improvements	20 – 40 years
Building	20 – 40 years
Leasehold Improvements	10 – 20 years
Equipment and Fixtures	5 – 10 years

e. Fiscal Year

The fiscal year ends on December 31.

f. Allocated Expenses

Expenses by function are directly allocated to programs. Other expenses are accumulated in the management and general cost center and allocated to programs.

g. Patient Fee Revenues

All patient fees earned by the Charities are retained within the organization and used to offset the operating expenses.

2. INVESTMENTS

Investments are carried at market value. Income, dividends, realized and unrealized gains and losses are reflected in the statement of activities. The organization invests cash in excess of daily requirements in short-term money market funds.

3. LEASE COMMITMENTS

At December 31, 2007, the Charities was obligated under rental leases for storefront clinic space in several locations. These leases do not meet the criteria for capitalization and are classified as operating leases with the related expenses charged to operations as incurred.

The following is a schedule by year of future minimum lease payments under operating leases as of December 31, 2007, that have initial or remaining lease terms in excess of one year.

Year Ended December 31	Minimum Lease Payments
2008	$500,000
2009	$460,000
2010	$425,000
2011	$360,000
2012	$315,000

4. SUBSEQUENT EVENT

On January 14, 2008, the Charities was awarded a $5,000,000 grant to inaugurate a new mental health program within its primary service area. The grant is primarily to be used to build a new facility to consolidate a number of its programs.

in the nonprofit world would translate to increased donor confidence and community support. In addition, many companies have found that compliance has improved their processes and systems, eliminated redundancies, improved the control environment, enhanced performance, and increased understanding of risk intelligence and corporate governance.[10] Even if the adoption of all SOX clauses may not be legally required for all nonprofits, periodic assessment of the organization's internal processes and financial controls should be on the agenda of every board.

TIPS FOR BOARD MEMBERS

1. Request that management show cash to the board in a trended monthly format (preferably as a graph) to highlight the movement of the organization's cash balances.

2. If accounts receivable or promises to give are a major portion of your organization's balance sheet, ask the organization's finance division to summarize its effort to maximize cash collections and to minimize bad debts and write-offs. Also request that it provides the policy for classifying purchases as capital assets and for depreciating them.

3. Examine the most recent footnotes to the financial statements and discuss with the auditors any significant issues.

4. Analyze with senior management the benefits and costs of adopting SOX-like procedures. Discuss with the auditors the changes that would need to be made under the adoption.

---

10. "Time for a second look at SOX compliance," by John T. Bigalke and Steven J. Burrill, *HFM* magazine, August 2007, page 57.

5.

Comparing Interim to Audited Financial Statements

FINANCIAL INFORMATION

As stated earlier, the board's fiduciary responsibilities necessitate that financial information be provided to it on an interim basis (monthly or quarterly). The board has the right to request from management that the interim statement be reported in the format it prefers. However, most boards have found that needless problems are created if the interim information is not given to them in substantially the same format as the year-end audited financial statements.

The main reason for this is that the year-end statements must be reported in conformance with generally accepted accounting principles (GAAP) and in accordance with generally accepted auditing standards (GAAS). If the interim statements do not also comply with those principles, then crucial information may be omitted from those reports to the board and the board may find itself unhappily surprised by information in the year-end statements.

There may be plausible reasons for the interim financial statements to the board to be different in some respects from the year-end GAAP format. Not everyone agrees at all times with all GAAP methodology. Although GAAP is developed by industry professionals and is designed to represent an organization's financial information in the least confusing manner, this may not always be the case.

For example, GAAP stipulates that interest income earned on short-term and long-term investment assets be reported as non-operating revenues. This means that an organization's operating margin will be reduced by the amount of the interest expense (although the net margin will reflect the higher earnings represented by the interest income). This will be the case in most nonprofit organizations that provide programmatic services, and therefore where investment income returns are not the primary mission.

In that case, some board members might prefer for their own clarification that (1) the interim statement of activities be reported with the interest income shown in the revenues section, or alternatively, (2) the interest expense be offset against the interest income and the "net" amount be reported as interest income in the non-operating section. (See Exhibit 7.) This isolates for the board the "true" operating margin results with both sides of the interest equation factored out.

In general, it is appropriate and permissible for the board to request presentation of the interim statements in whatever manner and format enhances their understanding. Still, the key concept should be that, if interim statements are presented that do not conform to GAAP, then an additional statement should be prepared and presented

Exhibit 7

ABC Charities, Inc.
Comparison of Statements of Activities
For the Year-to-Date Ending December 31, 2007
(in thousands)

	FORMAT		
	Audit (GAAP) 2007	**Interim #1 2007**	**Interim #2 2007**
PUBLIC SUPPORT AND REVENUE			
Service Revenues	53,600	53,600	53,600
Contributions	9,700	9,700	9,700
Grants	3,400	3,400	3,400
Investment Income	-	1,200	-
Total Support and Revenue	66,700	67,900	66,700
EXPENSES			
Program Services	47,600	47,600	47,600
Management and General	13,190	13,190	11,990
Fundraising	710	710	710
Total Expenses	61,500	61,500	60,300
Excess of Support and Revenue over Expenses (Operating Margin)	5,200	6,400	6,400
NON-OPERATING INCOME			
Gain/(Loss) on investments	1,200	-	-
Total Non-Operating Income	1,200	-	-
Excess of Support and Total Revenue over Expenses (Total Margin)	6,400	6,400	6,400
Net Assets, Beginning of Year	65,000	65,000	65,000
Change in net unrealized gains and losses on investments	(1,000)	(1,000)	(1,000)
Net Assets, End of Year	70,400	70,400	70,400

that *does* conform to GAAP. In this way, the board will be kept fully informed and will not be surprised by the year-end audit results.

In addition, effective for years ended after 12/15/2006, Statement of Auditing Standards 112 (SAS 112) changed the term and definition of reportable condition (what the auditor found while performing the audit) to management and those charged with governance. Under the new guidelines, "Significant Control Deficiencies" (SCD) are defined as any material deviation from GAAP and must be reported. For example, under the old rules, if the auditor came in and noted that the new office lease for the organization was not properly accounted for under GAAP, the auditors could propose an adjustment to correct the materially incorrect financials. Because this type of transaction happens with relative infrequency (say a 10-year lease) but is a part of GAAP, many accounting managers may not be aware of the proper accounting. In these cases, the auditor might determine that, in his professional judgment, this entry did not need to be reported to the Audit Committee. Now, with the new term and definition of SCD, the threshold has been lowered and the auditor must include any such material deviation from GAAP (i.e., one that requires an entry to be made to the financial statements) to be an SCD and reportable to the governing body.

STATISTICAL INFORMATION

Interestingly, GAAP does not require that any statistical information be reported in the body of the financial statements or in the footnotes. Statistical information certainly can enhance the reader's awareness of a variety of issues that may not be conveyed with only the financial information. For example, a foundation is not required to report the number of grants that it approved during the year. Yet this information could be very relevant because the gross number of grants may likely have some bearing or influence on the amount of grant funds that were approved. The information becomes even more important when it is reported as a ratio across time.

Box 4

SAMPLE STATISTICAL INFORMATION

	2005	2006	2007
Grant Dollars Approved	$1,000,000	$1,500,000	$2,000,000
Number of Grants Approved	100	160	250
Average Dollars per Approved Grant	$10,000	$9,375	$8,000

So, as addenda to the interim financial reports, the board may want to consider requesting of management statistical analyses or summaries that may further illuminate the operations of the nonprofit for board members. The information in Box 4, for example, provides a foundation's board with certain insights that would otherwise have been unavailable in the financial statements, and helps to develop conclusions that otherwise would not have been obtainable. A board member might observe from the information in Box 4 that, although the nonprofit organization paid out more funds in the two years since 2005, the amount of dollars approved per grant declined each year. Board members, donors, or potential donors may be vitally interested in the trend of dollars per approved grant. If this is the case, then the board should be receiving this type of information regularly. Yet without a request to management for such an analysis, it would be unobtainable from the financial statements. Some statistical information, and the ratios derived from them, may be more critical in the board's evaluation of management's performance than even the financial statements, and so should be highlighted in the board's interim financial and operational reports to the board.

TIPS FOR BOARD MEMBERS

1. Request that management present the interim monthly financial statements, particularly the balance sheet and the income statement, in the same format as the year-end audited financial statement. If management does so, any differences between the final year-end interim and audited statements will be easily identified.

2. Management and board members should determine what additional statistical information would be most useful to the board and would best elucidate progress toward achievement of the group's mission (critical success factors).

6.

Using Financial Information To Meet Other Reporting Requirements

It is crucial that the board have a full understanding of the information that is in an organization's financial statements for another reason: The financial statements are used as the basis for other important public reports, both required and optional. There are three in particular that boards should be aware of: the IRS Form 990, state charitable reports, and private charitable rating organization reports.

IRS FORM 990

Nonprofit organizations that have applied for and been approved by the IRS under Section 501(c) are, of course, exempt from most federal taxes (see Chapter 2). Nevertheless, they are still required by law to file an *informational form* with the IRS annually. This document is titled the Form 990.

There are several major elements of Form 990: The organization is required to report its revenues and expenses, its statement of financial position (balance sheet), and its statement of functional expenses. The data for these sections are usually taken from the audited financial statements of the organization. In addition, the form requires and thus provides an opportunity for the organization to introduce its programs and services to the reader.

The Form 990 also requires information on compensation paid to the officers, directors, trustees, and the chief executive officer, as well as the compensation of the five highest-paid employees who are not in the previous group. Also, the amounts paid to the five highest-paid nonsalaried individuals or companies must also be disclosed.

Because of the importance of the Form 990 to preserving the organization's federal tax-exempt status, at least one board member, presumably from the finance committee, should review the questions before the form is submitted. This oversight is necessary to ensure that the most accurate information is submitted to the IRS. In fact, best practice would dictate that the finance expert on the board review the entire return. In addition, some auditing firms are submitting the Form 990 to the entire board or committee with the audit and going through the form with them as they go through the SAS 61 report (now SAS 114), the financial statements, and the report to the board or management letter.

In addition to accuracy, nonprofit organizations need to ensure proper explanations, where necessary, of their financial results, as reported on Form 990. For example, an organization that is saving and building its cash reserves to finance the purchase of a new facility (from which to run its programs) may have accumulated significant reserves. As such, although the amount of the reserves and the related investment accounts may be accurate, management or the board may have concerns that funders will look at this information and think that the organization does not need the grant that they are requesting. Some explanation (not required by the IRS on Form 990) put onto the form in key locations could be very helpful in further explaining the rationale for such large reserves. This could ensure potential funders of the continued need for funds and present management in a more responsible light.

For the first time in many years, the IRS is updating and expanding the Form 990. The changes make it clear that the IRS is seeking to use the Form 990 as a means of learning more about the interests and relationships of board members of tax-exempt organizations and of identifying the potential for conflicts and bias between related boards.

Some of the more noteworthy changes that will be required for forms filed by organizations for their fiscal year beginning 2008 include

- Expanded definitions and disclosure of the family and business relationships of officers, directors, trustees, and key employees.

- Questions on executive compensation details regarding loans, executive perquisites, deferred compensation, and other retirement benefits; related organizations; and corporate governance.

- New reporting of compensation and benefits paid to officers, directors, trustees, and key employees of related organizations.

- New reporting of compensation and benefits payable to so-called "disqualified" persons.

- New disclosure requirements (required by the Pension Protection Act of 2006) relating to transfers to and from controlled entities.

STATE CHARITABLE REPORTS

A nonprofit that is active in a state will most likely be required to register and report annually to that state government, usually the Secretary of State's office. (Presently, only 10 states have no registration or reporting requirement for nonprofits.) Whether a nonprofit is "active" within a state usually requires some minimum of activity — but in most states that can be as little as soliciting a contribution by mail or Internet from any resident of the state. Therefore, many nonprofits find it necessary to register and report in more than one state.

Usually an organization's audited financial statements will provide most or all of the information that is required to be reported, or the reporting requirement may be satisfied by simply filing the group's audited financial statements with the state. Many states have also made it easier for multistate filers by adopting the Uniform Registration Form, which standardizes the information requested by those states. But whether a nonprofit is active in one or all 50 states, it is important for its board to be aware that it very likely has a state reporting burden (and some major cities have similar requirements).

CHARITABLE ORGANIZATION RATING GROUPS

There is another reason to provide a Form 990 to the government that has the most accurate and comprehensive data. Unlike individual income tax forms, the Form 990 is considered an *informational* report. Therefore, unlike individual tax forms whose confidentiality is strictly guarded by law from public disclosure, the Form 990 is available to anyone who requests it from the IRS. Or it may be requested directly from the nonprofit organization and must, by law, be provided within a short period of time.

The Internet has also made the Form 990's information even more publicly accessible. Since the late 1990s, Philanthropic Research, Inc., a 501(c)(3) public charity founded in 1994, has compiled on its Web site, GuideStar, more than 1 million Form 990s filed by IRS-recognized nonprofit organizations. Likewise, the Better Business Bureau's Wise Giving Alliance takes information from the Form 990 and financial statements and publishes it online and in print in its Wise Giving Guide. (The Wise Giving Alliance and GuideStar, which are private, non-government groups, also make evaluations and ratings of charitable organizations based on their own sometimes-controversial ratios and metrics of the financial information.)

With the click of a mouse, the financial and other supplemental information of many nonprofits is now available to most people, including sensitive salary and other data. For this reason, it is prudent for all board members to review the information filed with federal and state agencies, and to be aware of what charitable rating groups may be saying about their organization.

TIPS FOR BOARD MEMBERS

1. One or more board members should meet with the CFO and CEO (or auditors) to review each year's Form 990 and to discuss the upcoming form changes and any potential impacts on the organization.

2. Board members should visit charitable rating Web sites and learn what (if anything) is being written there about their organization. See www.guidestar.org and www.bbb.org.

7.

Using Financial Information To Evaluate Organizational Performance

RATIO ANALYSIS

One of the board's primary duties is to monitor the operational performance of management. The best way to do this is through the reporting and review of financial, statistical, and operational information. Earlier, the discussion and explanation of the formal financial statements ensured that board members would have an understanding of those basic documents. However, data in the financial statements should be utilized as the basis for additional assessment, through *ratio analysis*, which will provide the board with further vital information in determining whether management's goals are being met.

Ratio analysis is a method for taking two or more informational elements and utilizing them together to obtain additional information. Financial ratio analysis is the technique used to assess financial condition. There are a number of financial statement ratios that boards will find useful, if reported to them at least monthly (or quarterly, for smaller nonprofits). Box 5 shows the most common ratios that are available to the board for regular, periodic reporting by management. Each board will need to determine the value of any particular ratio based on the nonprofit's particular industry group, sources of funding, types of expenses, level of debt, amount of investments, and size of fixed assets.

Box 5

RATIOS POTENTIALLY USEFUL TO BOARD MEMBERS

- Current Ratio
- Quick Ratio
- Days Cash on Hand
- Days in Accounts Receivable
- Average Payment Period
- Average Age of Plant
- Debt Service Coverage

- Return on Net Assets
- Operating Margin Percentage
- Net Margin Percentage
- Interest Expense Percentage
- Interest Income Percentage
- Program Spending Ratio
- Fundraising Ratio

CURRENT RATIO

The *current ratio*, which computes the organization's ability to meet its current obligations, is one of the most commonly used in all nonprofit sectors to measure liquidity. It measures the number of dollars held in current assets as a percentage of the dollars owed in current liabilities. A result of 1.0 means that the organization has exactly enough current assets (assets that are convertible to cash within a short period of time, usually within one year) to pay off all of its current liabilities (liabilities that are payable within a short period of time, usually within one year).

A healthy ratio for most organizations will be in the 2.0 to 4.0 range. That level will assure any reader that the organization is financially solvent, having double to quadruple the financial means, in the near term, to pay off its short-term liabilities.

The current ratio is expressed in the following equation:

$$\frac{\text{Current Assets}}{\text{Current Liabilities}}$$

(For example: $22,800 / $7,500 = 3.04 current ratio)

QUICK RATIO

The *quick ratio* is an adjunct to the current ratio. It is also known as the asset-test ratio because it measures the organization's ability to meet short-term obligations from its most liquid, or quick, assets. Quick assets are defined as cash or assets quickly and easily convertible into cash, such as marketable securities and accounts receivable (but not inventory or other assets that may take some time and effort to convert to cash). Like the current ratio, a range between 2.0 and 4.0 would be considered healthy.

The quick ratio is expressed in the following equation:

$$\frac{\text{Cash} + \text{Cash Equivalent} + \text{Accounts Receivable} + \text{Unconditional Promises To Pay}}{\text{Current Liabilities}}$$

(For example: $21,900 / $7,500 = 2.92 quick ratio)

DAYS CASH ON HAND

This may be the most important of all the ratios for board members. *Days cash on hand* measures the number of days of average cash expenses that the organization maintains. The ratio can be expressed in terms of either days cash on hand *in short-term sources* or *in all sources*. Like the current ratio, a higher value will always be preferred. The board will be able to assess the organization's ability to meet its financial obligations based on the outcomes from this ratio.

The two ratios of days cash on hand are shown in the following equations:

1) Days Cash on Hand (*Short-Term Sources*) =

$$\frac{\text{Cash + Short-Term Investments}}{(\text{Total Expenses} - \text{Depreciation}) / 365}$$

(For example: $1,200 + $6,500 / (($61,500 − $3,200) / 365)
= 48.2 days cash on hand)

2) Days Cash on Hand (*All Sources*) =

$$\frac{\text{Cash + Short-Term Investments + All Long-Term Investments}}{(\text{Total Expenses} - \text{Depreciation}) / 365}$$

(For example: $1,200 + $6,500 + $62,300 + $10,000 / (($61,500 − $3,200)
/ 365) = 500.8 days cash on hand)

It should be noted that cash from short-term or all sources may include cash from temporarily restricted sources, which is generally not available to meet current obligations due to its restrictions. Thus, it is possible for this ratio to overstate the organization's ability to meet its basic operating needs. For ratio purposes, the board may want to exclude restricted cash from this equation.

DAYS IN ACCOUNTS RECEIVABLE

Days in accounts receivable is a critical ratio, particularly in those nonprofits that provide fee-based client services. It measures the average time that receivables are outstanding, and is also known as the *average collection period*. Higher ratio results lead to fewer days cash on hand and potentially to greater short-term financing requirement. Management should always strive to keep the days in accounts receivable ratio as low as possible. Although nonprofit organizations exist in many different industries with many different processes and procedures for this ubiquitous ratio, 30 days is a solid benchmark.

The days in accounts receivable ratio is expressed in the following equation:

$$\frac{\text{Net Accounts Receivable}}{\text{Net Service Revenues} / 365}$$

(For example: $9,200 / ($53,600 / 365) = 62.65 days in accounts receivable)

AVERAGE PAYMENT PERIOD

The *average payment period* ratio is the flip side of days in accounts receivable. It measures the average time that elapses before the organization's current liabilities are paid. High values may indicate potential liquidity problems, particularly if there is a low number of days cash on hand. Low values may indicate that invoices are paid too quickly.

The average payment period ratio is expressed in the following equation:

$$\frac{\text{Current Liabilities}}{(\text{Total Expenses} - \text{Depreciation}) / 365}$$

(For example: $7,500 / (($61,500 – $3,200) / 365) = 46.9 days average payment period)

AVERAGE AGE OF PLANT

This is a very important ratio for those nonprofit organizations that own substantial fixed assets, particularly buildings and equipment. *Average age of plant* measures the average age in years of the organization's fixed assets. Values between 5.0 and 9.0 years usually indicate a relatively young plant with all of its equipment, new and old. Each industry will have its own benchmark and these should be known and used appropriately. The importance to a nonprofit of this ratio is that lower numbers may indicate newer, better facilities and equipment that will typically enhance client satisfaction, while higher results may indicate the opposite — as well as the need to begin planning for the financing and replacement of older fixed assets.

The average age of plant ratio is expressed in the following equation:

$$\frac{\text{Accumulated Depreciation}}{\text{Depreciation Expenses}}$$

(For example: $18,000 / $3,000 = 6.0 average age of plant)

DEBT SERVICE COVERAGE

The *debt service coverage* ratio is a key ratio used by investment managers, banks, and bond rating agencies to determine the organization's ability to pay back its bond debt, mortgages, or other borrowings. It measures the relationship between the organization's bottom line cash and its annual debt service payments (principal + interest expense). A higher ratio, typically between 2.0 and 5.0, is preferred as it indicates a higher level of profitability compared to its debt obligations.

The debt service coverage ratio is expressed in the following equation:

$$\frac{\text{Excess of Support and Total Revenues over Expenses} + \text{Depreciation} + \text{Interest Expense}}{\text{Principal Payments} + \text{Interest Expense}}$$

(For example: ($6,400 + $3,000 + $3,200) / ($1,500 + $3,200) = 2.68 debt service coverage)

RETURN ON NET ASSETS

This is a profitability ratio that is used to determine the organization's return of total margin compared to its unrestricted net assets, expressed as a percentage. The ratio measures the ability to fund additions, renovations, and new program initiatives without having to add new debt. The higher the result, the better.

The return on net assets ratio is expressed in the following equation:

$$\frac{\text{Excess of Support and Total Revenues over Expenses}}{\text{Unrestricted Net Assets}}$$

(For example: $6,400 / $32,600 = 19.6% return on net assets)

OPERATING MARGIN PERCENTAGE

Operating margin percentage is a useful ratio because it measures the organization's bottom line (before non-operating revenues), compared to its total revenues. The computed ratio allows the reader to quickly, and rather accurately, determine the extent of the organization's profitability on its core operations. Higher values are preferable.

The operating margin percentage ratio is expressed in the following equation:

$$\frac{\text{Excess of Support and Revenues over Expenses}}{\text{Total Support and Revenues}}$$

(For example: $5,200 / $66,700 = 7.8% operating margin)

NET MARGIN PERCENTAGE

Similar to the operating margin percentage ratio, the *net* (or *total*) *margin percentage* measures profitability based on *all* revenues, including non-operating revenues. This typically means investment income is included, although it is generally classified as non-operating and is reported below the operating margin (excess of operating revenues over expenses). Higher margins are preferred as a result of this calculation.

The net margin percentage ratio is expressed in the following equation:

$$\frac{\text{Excess of Support and Total Revenues over Expenses}}{\text{Total Support and Revenues}}$$

(For example: $6,400 / $66,700 = 9.6% net margin)

INTEREST EXPENSE PERCENTAGE

The board may be interested in the rate being paid on its borrowed money, particularly if the amounts are large. The *interest expense percentage ratio* measures the overall average interest rate being paid by the organization to finance its long-term debt. It allows the board to determine whether the current rate is sustainable and competitive or whether refinancing should be explored.

The interest expense percentage ratio is expressed in the following equation:

$$\frac{\text{Total Interest Expense}}{\text{Current and Long-Term Bond Debt}}$$

(For example: $3,200 / ($1,500 + $64,800) = 4.8% interest expense)

INTEREST INCOME PERCENTAGE

In contrast to the interest expense percentage ratio, the *interest income percentage* measures the overall average percentage earnings on all of the organization's assets with potential to be invested. It allows the board to quickly evaluate overall investment returns, which may be useful in future investment decision making.

The interest income percentage ratio is expressed in the following equation:

$$\frac{\text{Total Interest Income} + \text{Dividend Income} + \text{Realized Gains on Securities}}{\text{Cash} + \text{Cash Equivalent} + \text{All Long-Term Investments}}$$

(For example: $1,200 / ($1,200 + $6,500 + $62,300 + $10,000)
= 1.5% interest income)

PROGRAM SPENDING RATIO

The *program spending ratio* allows directors to see the percentage that a nonprofit is spending on programs compared to how much it is spending on fundraising and administration. A higher number is always better; charity groups typically recommend at least 65 percent.

The program spending ratio is expressed in the following equation:

$$\frac{\text{Program Expense}}{\text{Total Exenses}}$$

(For example: $40,6000 / $61,500 = 66.01% program spending ratio)

In recent years, the program spending ratio has taken on added importance because more outsiders — donors, charity rating groups, and regulators — are focusing on it as a primary indicator of whether a nonprofit is using its funds wisely and efficiently to further its mission — or spending too much on nonprogram activities. The board of any nonprofit whose program spending ratio falls below 65 percent had better discuss with management and auditors the reason(s) for the low ratio. One reason, for example could be that expenses are not being accurately and appropriately allocated in the audited financial statements between program activities and management and general or fundraising.

FUNDRAISING RATIO

Like the program spending ratio, the fundraising ratio is being closely observed by many donors and outside groups. The fundraising ratio's purpose is to provide a quick, easy, and understandable view of the percentage of dollars being spent to raise a nonprofit's contributions and grant revenue. If the percentage is high, then questions should be raised by the board about whether fundraising activities are too "inefficient" (i.e., too much of each donation is being spent to obtain it) — and whether the dollars raised by the nonprofit are really being used to benefit its clientele and achieve its programmatic mission. If the percentage is low, donors, outsiders, and the board may be more assured that contributions and grants are being put to their intended use on program activities. Analysis should always be ongoing. It should be noted that in 2002 the IRS started to send out "educational" letters to those nonprofit organizations that had contribution revenue but little or no (or proportionately low) fundraising expenses. These letters said the nonprofit organization should give this area another look while the IRS would continue to monitor this in the future.

The fundraising ratio is expressed in the following equation:

$$\frac{\text{Fundraising Expenses}}{\text{Contribution Revenue} + \text{Grant Revenue}}$$

(For example: $710 / ($9,000 + $3,400) = 5.73\%$ fundraising ratio)

A nonprofit fundraising ratio that exceeds 20 – 30 percent should alert the board that it needs to discuss the reasons for this with management and auditors — and be prepared to explain publicly the reasons for a high ratio.[11]

Interestingly, while these ratios have value in the determining some financial and operational outcomes, a *Wall Street Journal* article, published in 2007, points out that donors, "especially younger, business-minded ones, now tend to want more information on how successful a charity's programs are in addressing the issues the charity sets out to resolve, from feeding the homeless to securing employment for the disabled... The problem is, it can be difficult — and expensive — to measure whether charitable programs are actually working, and most nonprofits aren't willing to devote scarce resources to collecting such information."[12]

Thus, the article concludes with several very useful suggestions for potential donors to nonprofit organizations, as follows: "It's also smart to see if the charity's progress has ever been evaluated by a third party, rather than just the charity itself. Check the charity's Web site or annual report for specific details on how it gauges its results. If the information isn't there, call the charity and ask. Be wary about giving, however, if a charity doesn't answer your questions or provide annual reports or other filings.

---

11. There may, in fact, be many legitimate reasons for a high fundraising ratio. For example, a newly founded nonprofit may need to spend proportionately more than other established groups to raise donations and grants in its early years, and this may result in a high ratio in the first years of its operation. In any case, the board should be prepared to justify and explain a high ratio to any inquirers.

12. "Doing Due Diligence on Your Donations," Rachel Emma Silverman and Sally Beatty, *Wall Street Journal*, 12/20/07, page D1. Reprinted by permission of Wall Street Journal ©2007 Dow Jones & Company, Inc. All rights reserved Worldwide. License number #1874800753127.

Another way to learn about a charity: Volunteer with the group, or visit a site to get to know staffers, clients and facilities."

Nonprofit boards and their senior management need to be aware of these tips that are being given to potential donors and make sure that their books and records are able to support these types of donor information requests.

TIPS FOR BOARD MEMBERS

The ratios described above are the basic ones that may be of use to a nonprofit board and which it should expect to see on a regular basis from management. Over time, board members will be able to determine which are the most important to them — because they provide critical and substantial information about the organization's operations and its ability to further its mission — and what additional ratio analysis might be useful. Conversations with management and auditors to determine the appropriate metrics are more than worth the time they take for board members.

8.

Advanced Methods of Measuring Organizational Performance

In earlier chapters, some advanced analysis techniques were referenced, such as *trending* and *benchmarks*, particularly with respect to ratios. This chapter will define those concepts in more detail, show how they can enhance statistical and ratio analysis, and then discuss the *balanced scorecard*, an analysis technique that integrates financial information with other types of analysis to help board members determine in a more comprehensive way if management is moving toward achieving its goals and if progress is being made in furthering the organization's mission.

TRENDING

Trending refers to the display and analysis of data or information across time. Without trending, board members will only have a snapshot of one particular moment of an organization's financial and other data. The use of trending greatly enhances the board's understanding of the directions in which an organization is heading.

Take, for example, one of the important financial ratios identified in Chapter 7, days cash on hand (all sources). A good interim financial report would include this ratio and directors would be able to observe as in Exhibit 8 that the 2007 *days cash on hand (all sources)* was 499.15 days. This ratio indicates to the board that the organization is in a strong position to meet its financial obligations.

But is this the entire story? A better interim financial report would also include ratios from prior years and a narrative explanation, to enable the board to observe and understand the direction and trend of cash on hand. From Exhibit 8, for example, a board could quickly grasp any trends that may be relevant over the past five years — for example, although cash on hand is an excellent ratio today, is this a decline from prior years? Does that indicate a trend that the board needs to be concerned about? An accompanying narrative would address any trends and explain unusual data, such as the substantial increase in cash in 2005 in Exhibit 8.

Trending is often more easily understood in well-designed graphs, charts, and tables than in raw numbers or narrative explanations. Board members should ask management to provide graphs and charts routinely to illustrate the essential elements of financial performance.

BENCHMARKS

Benchmarking is another useful management technique. It requires an organization to compare its ratios, trends, and analysis, both financial and nonfinancial, with those of its peers. Benchmarking enables a board to determine whether a nonprofit is operating and performing at a level that comports with similar organizations.

Let's take a concrete look at benchmarking with the following *debt service coverage ratio* example (Exhibit 9). Debt service coverage (see Chapter 7) measures the relationship between the organization's bottom line cash and its annual debt service payments (principal + interest expense). This indicates the organization's ability to pay back its bonds, mortgages, or other long-term debts. A higher ratio is preferred.

Without the organization's historic debt service ratio data the board will only know that the ratio for 2007 was 2.68. However, if the ratios for the previous four years are also shown, it becomes immediately obvious that, prior to 2005, the organization's annual ratio was much higher. As stated above, this trending is most easily grasped when plotted on a graph or chart (see Exhibit 9). Without other data, the chart

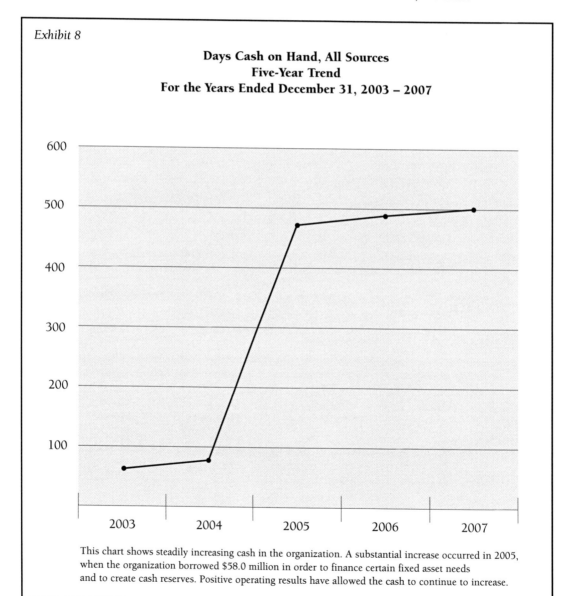

Exhibit 8

Days Cash on Hand, All Sources
Five-Year Trend
For the Years Ended December 31, 2003 – 2007

This chart shows steadily increasing cash in the organization. A substantial increase occurred in 2005, when the organization borrowed $58.0 million in order to finance certain fixed asset needs and to create cash reserves. Positive operating results have allowed the cash to continue to increase.

indicates a significant decline in the debt service coverage ratio and therefore a reduced ability to borrow additional funds in the future.

But is this the whole story? Not necessarily. For example, perhaps the ratios of the earlier years were much higher than other organizations in the group's nonprofit sector. Or higher than that considered acceptable or optimal by lenders or bond-rating agencies. To learn that important information, it is necessary to additionally plot the average (or possibly median) of the debt service ratios of a group of organizations in the nonprofit's sector that perform similar functions (and which have also borrowed funds), as shown in Exhibit 9.

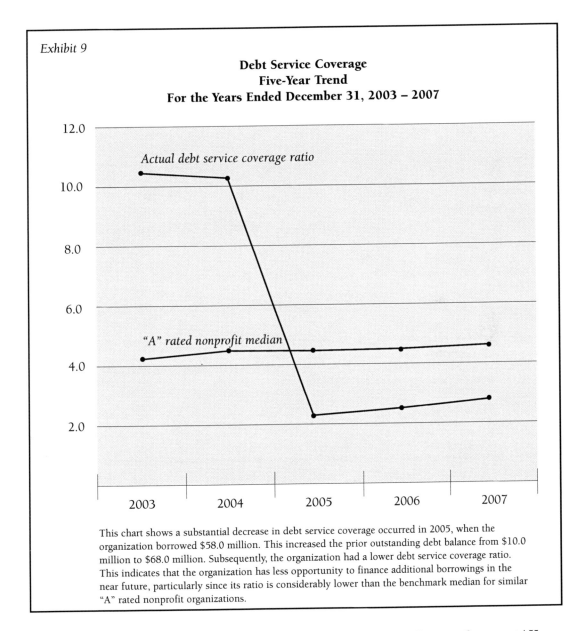

Exhibit 9

Debt Service Coverage
Five-Year Trend
For the Years Ended December 31, 2003 – 2007

Actual debt service coverage ratio

"A" rated nonprofit median

This chart shows a substantial decrease in debt service coverage occurred in 2005, when the organization borrowed $58.0 million. This increased the prior outstanding debt balance from $10.0 million to $68.0 million. Subsequently, the organization had a lower debt service coverage ratio. This indicates that the organization has less opportunity to finance additional borrowings in the near future, particularly since its ratio is considerably lower than the benchmark median for similar "A" rated nonprofit organizations.

With the addition of the second plot, the board is able to see significant variances between its nonprofit's ratio and those of other, similarly situated organizations. Exhibit 9 shows that, while there was a precipitous drop of the debt service ratio in 2005, it is not as significant or threatening when compared with the average ratios of other organizations. Still, the chart indicates a variance and shows the board the value its nonprofit needs to strive for. Exhibit 9 can provide valuable information for the board, management, lenders, and bond-rating agencies. And benchmarking charts like Exhibit 9 for other important ratios can likewise provide essential additional analysis of other elements of the financial statements.

BALANCED SCORECARD

There is an additional management tool that enables the board to gain an even better understanding of the organization's operations as a whole — the *balanced scorecard*. Balanced scorecards have gained acceptance over the past decade for their ability to paint a relatively complete picture of organizational performance. Scorecards take into account the key financial elements, as described in chapters above, as well as other key elements that drive the outcomes mandated by the board. The exhibits in this section show one of the many ways to present this information.

The scorecard is simply a means by which the organization can keep track of its outcomes as compared to its goals. It "provides executives with a comprehensive framework that translates a company's vision and strategy into a coherent set of performance measures" that can be communicated to the various stakeholders in the nonprofit.[13] Furthermore, "the balanced scorecard retains financial measurement as a critical summary of managerial and business performance, but it highlights a more general and integrated set of measurements that link customer, internal process, employee, and system performance to long-term financial success."[14]

The balanced scorecard utilizes four different quadrants of performance measures to create a natural and continuous feedback loop that can then be used to monitor and improve the organization's level of effectiveness. The four quadrants are

- Financial Perspective

- Customer Perspective

- Internal Perspective

- Learning and Growth

An organization may use different performance measures within each of the four groupings. Box 6 lists some of the more common considerations that are utilized for each quadrant. Once again, keep in mind that each organization must use those items that represent its own particular and unique critical success factors.

---

13. *The Balanced Scorecard*, Kaplan and Norton, Harvard Business School Press, 1996, page 24.

14. Ibid., page 21.

BALANCED SCORECARD QUADRANTS

FINANCIAL PERSPECTIVE

- Return on Capital
- Competitive Position
- Volume Growth
- Reduced Cash Outlays
- Improved Cash Receipts

CUSTOMER PERSPECTIVE

- Customer Satisfaction
- Employee Satisfaction
- Funder Satisfaction

INTERNAL PERSPECTIVE

- Product Innovation
- Perfect Orders (reduce errors)

LEARNING AND GROWTH

- Strategic Awareness
- Mandated Hours of Education per Employee

Initially, it may appear that balanced scorecards are only useful for larger nonprofits, or for those nonprofits that have major competitors, both for-profit and nonprofit. However, that is not the case. All nonprofits can benefit from the disciplined review required by the balanced scorecard of the mission, goals, and strategies of the nonprofit.

HOW TO DEVELOP A SCORECARD

There are several ways to develop a balanced scorecard, including

- Developing an executable organizational "business" strategy by outlining the important elements that will make the nonprofit successful.

- Describing the strategy for users and employees to enhance their understanding and encourage their buy-in.

- Designing and developing the scorecard framework with objectives and performance measurements that closely follow the strategic objectives outlined by the organization.

A scorecard does not stand alone as an unrelated set of metrics. Instead, it integrates the financial and nonfinancial goals and establishes a monitoring system to ensure the organization's desired outcomes are achieved.

Exhibit 10

Brilliant Hospital
Balanced Scorecard

HEALTHCARE INSIGHTS

Financial Perspective . . . .**2.19** **Needs Improvement**

Return on Net Assets . . . .**3.60** **Needs Improvement**

Competitive Position	0.83	Unsatisfactory
Volume Growth	1.00	*Poor*
Reduced Cash Outlays	3.50	Good
Improved Cash Receipts	2.00	**Needs Improvement**

Customer Perspective . . . .**2.20** **Needs Improvement**

Patient Satisfaction Surveys	2.05	**Needs Improvement**
Employee Satisfaction Surveys	2.20	**Needs Improvement**
Physician Satisfaction Surveys	2.35	**Needs Improvement**

Internal Perspective . . . .**3.31** **Good**

Product Innovations	3.00	Good
Error Reductions	2.50	**Needs Improvement**
Quality Indicators	4.00	Very Good
Clinical Outcomes	3.75	Good

Learning and Growth Perspective . . . .**3.00** **Good**

Strategic Awareness	3.00	Good
Leadership Surveys	3.20	Good
Mandated Educational Hours per Employee	2.80	**Needs Improvement**

OVERALL PERFORMANCE:	**Score**	**Weight**	**Weighted Score**
Financial	2.19	0.25	0.547
Customer	2.20	0.25	0.550
Internal	3.31	0.25	0.828
Learning and Growth	3.00	0.25	0.750
TOTAL SCORE	2.675	Needs Improvement	

0 = Poor = lowest 10th percentile of the benchmark
1 = Unsatisfactory = 11th – 25th percentile of the benchmark
2 = Needs Improvement = 26th – 50th percentile of the benchmark
3 = Good = 51st – 75th percentile of the benchmark
4 = Very Good = 76th – 90th percentile of the benchmark
5 = Excellent = 91st – 100th percentile of the benchmark

Source: INSIGHTS decision-support management accountability software. www.hcillc.com

BALANCED SCORECARD IN NONPROFIT ORGANIZATIONS

Any nonprofit organization, regardless of what sector it is in, can benefit from utilizing the balanced scorecard. Exhibit 10 illustrates some of the specific elements that could and should be used in the measure of performance, for example, for a nonprofit hospital.

As can be observed in Exhibit 10, the factors considered go well beyond financial indicators, thereby allowing users to gain a more complete insight into the goals, achievements, and shortcomings of the organization. Financial and nonfinancial considerations are both critical in evaluating this nonprofit hospital, so it is crucial that the hospital sets goals for all, not just financial outcomes. (In fact, excelling in the nonfinancial elements is likely to buttress and enhance financial success.)

Further, the scorecard is only half completed when the organization describes its goals and measures performance against them. Exhibit 11, shows the organization's scorecard as compared to quadrant goals and measurements of other peer organizations, as indicated in the last column (with proprietary data from a benchmark service). It is important to obtain such data so the board can learn how its organization and management are performing relative to their peers. The future success of its nonprofit may well be based on the results of this peer analysis.

BALANCING THE SCORECARD

It will probably occur to the reader that not all quadrants and metrics will be equal for every organization. To some nonprofits, for example, the customer perspective may be more important to its mission and ultimate result than the internal perspective, and vice versa. Therefore, it is important for each organization to "balance" its scorecard by weighting the value of its own unique metrics. Through the process of balancing of the scorecard, an organization can determine and value its most important success criteria in an objective manner.

For most organizations, the scorecard will generally have a relative equal weight for the four quadrants, with no one quadrant having a disproportionate share of the total allocated to it. A balanced approach might be 30 percent each to financial and internal process and 20 percent each to customer perspective and learning and growth. On the other hand, an unbalanced scorecard might allocate 70 percent of the total to the financial quadrant, leaving only 30 percent for the other three. While this allocation may have a short-term benefit, in the long term it could have a deleterious impact on the organization's outcomes, financial and nonfinancial.

The balanced scorecard is an exceptional technique for enabling boards to promote excellence in management and achievement of its mission and goals.

Exhibit 11

Balanced Scorecard Drill Down
Financial Perspective
Aggregate Indicator: Return on Net Assets

Indicator	Positive Trend
Profitability	
Operating Margin	Up
Excess (Total) Margin	Up
EBIDA revenue	Up
EBIDA assets	Up
Return of Equity	Up
Liquidity	
Days Cash on Hand (All Sources)	Up
Current	Up
Days of Revenue in Accounts Receivable	Down
Average Payment Period	Down
Capital Structure	
Equity Financing	Up
Long-Term Debt to Capitalization	Down
Cash Flow to Total Debt	Up
Annual Debt Service Coverage	Up
Cushion	Up
Asset Efficiency	
Total Asset Turnover	Up
Inventory Turnover	Up
TOTAL RETURN ON NET ASSETS	

Source: INSIGHTS decision-support management accountability software. www.hcillc.com.

HEALTHCARE INSIGHTS

| PRIOR YEAR | | CURRENT YEAR | | |
Month	Year-to-Date	Month	Year-to-Date	Comparison to Benchmark
				.Good
0.04	0.05	0.04	0.05	*Very Good*
0.07	0.08	0.11	0.13	**EXCELLENT**
0.18	0.16	0.17	0.16	Good
0.08	0.07	0.12	0.11	Good
0.09	0.07	0.09	0.08	Good
				.Poor
224.00	227.00	234.00	240.00	**EXCELLENT**
1.1	1.1	1.2	1.2	Poor
82.00	91.00	85.00	86.00	Poor
110.00	112.00	105.00	107.00	Unsatisfactory
				.Poor
0.15	0.14	0.15	0.14	Poor
0.72	0.72	0.71	0.72	Needs Improvement
0.04	0.03	0.04	0.03	Poor
2.04	2.10	2.10	2.00	Poor
9.40	9.20	9.50	9.60	Good
				.Good
1.28	1.18	1.26	1.25	*Very Good*
14	15	15	16	Good
				Needs Improvement

Tips for Board Members

1. Determine what financial ratios are most pertinent and useful for the board and ask management to provide them in the interim (monthly or quarterly) financial report for the board's review. Request that it be presented to show any variances between actual and budgeted ratios and, where appropriate, between the nonprofit's ratios and those of its peers or sector.

2. Develop with management a balanced scorecard, and request that it be updated and presented to the board at appropriate times (monthly, quarterly, or semi-annually).[15] The balanced scorecard will include all of the vital operational elements that were previously agreed upon, and the comparison of these goals with actual results. Thus, the balanced scorecard provides the best summary of compliance (or noncompliance) with the board's approved financial and nonfinancial goals.

---

15. The board of an organization experiencing a number of troublesome areas may want to request the scorecard more, rather than less, frequently.

Conclusion

To most board members, fulfilling their fiduciary responsibilities in the financial area is the most difficult task they encounter as a director. It is our hope that this book has helped to make this a less daunting duty.

At the beginning, it was the stated goal of this book to give board members the ability to understand the basic financial documents that they will encounter — and to know what types of documents and information to request from the nonprofit's managers. Along the way, we have also provided advice on how to use that information to measure a nonprofit's progress toward meeting its mission and goals, in both financial and nonfinancial areas. A board that takes that guidance to heart and puts those recommendations into practice will have gone a long way toward meeting its most important fiduciary responsibilities.

Understanding Nonprofit Financial Statements has provided the basic financial building blocks. Now it's up to you to use them!

Appendix 1

SUPPLEMENTAL AUDITOR REPORTS

Nonprofit board members should be aware of two other reports that may be included in the auditor's annual report. These reports are intended to provide, when necessary, additional information to board members, allowing for greater understanding of management's performance in utilizing accounting principles and practices. These reports — (1) SAS 114 letter, and (2) Reports Required in Accordance with Office of Management and Budget Circular A-133 — are described below. Additionally, other supplemental information that may also be necessary is outlined.

SAS 114 LETTER

The American Institute of Certified Public Accountants' Statement on Auditing Standards No. 114 (SAS 114) — The Auditor's Communication with Those Charged with Governance requires communication of certain matters to the audit committee, or its equivalent, on an annual basis. The report, usually referred to as a *management letter*, is intended solely for the use of the board of directors and management. It is meant to highlight issues and concerns observed by the auditors that they wish to communicate to the board. Although there are more and more requests from outsiders who wish to see this report, the organization is the final authority on whether it chooses to release it. That decision will usually be governed in evaluating who is making the request.

Statement of Auditing Standards No. 114, *The Auditor's Communication with Those Charged with Governance*

Issue Date: December 19, 2006

Effective Date: This SAS is effective for periods beginning on or after December 15, 2006. Early application is permitted.

Executive Summary

Statement on Auditing Standards (SAS) No. 114 supersedes SAS No. 61, *Communication with Audit Committees*, as amended. This SAS establishes standards and provides guidance to an auditor on matters to be communicated with those charged with governance.

In the wake of well-publicized audit failures and emerging best practices in corporate governance, expectations have increased for auditors to communicate openly and candidly with those charged with governance regarding significant findings and issues related to the audit. The Auditing Standards Board (ASB) believes SAS is responsive to the issues and expectations in the U.S. nonissuer community and will improve audit practice and serve the public interest.

In developing this SAS, the ASB considered the communication requirements of the Proposed International Standard on Auditing 260 (Revised), *The Auditor's*

Communication with Those Charged with Governance, which was issued by the International Auditing and Assurance Standards Board in March 2005.

SAS No. 61 established communication requirements applicable to entities that either have an audit committee or that have otherwise formally designated oversight of the financial reporting process to a group equivalent to an audit committee. SAS No. 114 broadens the applicability of the SAS to audits of the financial statements of all nonissuers and establishes a requirement for the auditor to communicate with those charged with governance certain significant matters related to the audit.

The SAS uses the term *those charged with governance* to refer to those with responsibility for overseeing the strategic direction of the entity and obligations related to the accountability of the entity, including overseeing the entity's financial reporting process. It uses the term *management* to refer to those who are responsible for achieving the objectives of the enterprise and who have the authority to establish policies and make decisions by which those objectives are to be pursued. Management is responsible for the entity's financial statements.

The SAS identifies specific matters to be communicated, many of which are generally consistent with the requirements in SAS No. 61. However, the SAS includes certain additional matters to be communicated and provides additional guidance on the communication process.

In particular, the SAS:

- Describes the principal purposes of communication with those charged with governance and stresses the importance of effective two-way communication.

- Requires the auditor to determine the appropriate person(s) in the entity's governance structure with whom to communicate particular matters. That person may vary depending on the nature of the matter to be communicated.

- Recognizes the diversity in governance structures among entities (including the existence of audit committees or other subgroups charged with governance) and encourages the use of professional judgment in deciding with whom to communicate particular matters.

- Recognizes the unique considerations for communicating with those charged with governance when all of those charged with governance are involved in managing the entity, which may be the case with some small entities.

- Adds requirements to communicate

    - An overview of the planned scope and timing of the audit.

    - Representations the auditor is requesting from management.

- Provides additional guidance on the communication process, including the forms and timing of communication. Significant findings from the audit should be in writing when, in the auditor's professional judgment, oral communication would not be adequate. Other communications may be oral or in writing,

- Requires the auditor to evaluate the adequacy of the two-way communication between the auditor and those charged with governance.

- Establishes a requirement to document required communications with those charged with governance.

REPORTS REQUIRED IN ACCORDANCE WITH OFFICE OF MANAGEMENT AND BUDGET CIRCULAR A-133

If the organization receives federal funding over a certain threshold amount, it may be subject to an Office of Management and Budget (OMB) audit. This audit requires additional reporting as part of the financial reports to the audit committee or the board, including

- Independent Auditor's Report on Compliance and on Internal Control over Financial Reporting Based on an Audit of Financial Statements Performed in Accordance with Government Auditing Standards

- Independent Auditor's Report on Compliance with Requirements Applicable to Each Major Program and Internal Control over Compliance in Accordance with OMB Circular A-133

- Schedule of Expenditures of Federal Awards

- Notes to Schedule of Expenditures of Federal Awards

- Schedule of Findings and Questioned Costs

OTHER SUPPLEMENTAL INFORMATION

Management, the audit committee, or the board may request that other information or reports be included as part of the reports issued by the auditors. The supplemental information or reports are presented for purposes of additional analysis and are not a required part of the basic financial statements. Such information is often subject to the auditing procedures applied in the audit of the basic financial statements and the auditors will often state their opinion as to whether this information is fairly stated in all material respects in relation to the basic financial statements taken as a whole.

Examples of some commonly included supplemental reports and information are

- Consolidating statements

- Investment statistics

- Grant and contract summaries

TIPS FOR BOARD MEMBERS

1. The audit committee or board should ask the auditors if an SAS 114 management letter is necessary or required at the conclusion of every audit. If so, a copy should be provided to them.

2. If a management letter is issued by the auditor, the board should ensure that management has provided action plans to correct any of the issues discussed in the letter. The action plans should be included in the auditor's report and should include timetables for completions. Finally, the board should schedule time on the agenda of each meeting throughout the upcoming year to review the level of completion of each item in the action plan.

Appendix 2: Contents of the CD-ROM

The attached CD-ROM contains the electronic form of *Presenting: Nonprofit Financials: An Overview of Board Fiduciary Responsibility,* by Thomas A. McLaughlin. The tools on this CD-ROM are published by BoardSource and can be used as is or, in some cases, customized for your organization's needs. The purpose of this presentation is to familiarize board members — experienced and novice — with the financial information they need. Included in this presentation are definitions, job descriptions, and sample financial documents that will give board members an overview of the lines of responsibility within the organization and an understanding of how to assess a nonprofit's financial health.

The files on this CD-ROM are in four formats:

- Microsoft® PowerPoint® graphics presentation format (.ppt)

- Microsoft Word for Windows and Macintosh, version 6.0 (.doc)

- plain text format (.txt)

- Adobe PDF format, version 4.0 (.pdf)

The documents for each format are contained in the appropriately named subdirectory.

The CD-ROM is the copyright of BoardSource and is protected under federal copyright law. Any unlawful duplication of this CD-ROM is in violation of that copyright. Before customizing Microsoft Word or text documents, save a backup copy on your hard drive, and work from the copy on your hard drive.

Contents

Microsoft® PowerPoint® graphics presentation files

- *Presenting: Nonprofit Financials* presentation with talking points

Word files

- *Presenting: Nonprofit Financials* presentation text

- Talking points

Generic text files

- *Presenting: Nonprofit Financials* presentation text

- Talking points

Adobe PDF file

- Sample financial documents

The slides are in Microsoft® PowerPoint® graphics presentation format that can be used as an on-screen presentation or printed as overhead transparency slides or handouts for the board. The CD-ROM also contains additional generic text files with the same information that appears on the slides and in the presentation notes and talking points. Use some or all of the sections depending on how they apply to your nonprofit.

We hope you enjoy the flexibility and customization capabilities of electronic text. If you have any questions regarding the files on this CD-ROM, call BoardSource at 800-883-6262.

BoardSource
Suite 900
1828 L Street, NW
Washington, DC 20036-5104
202-452-6262
Fax 202-452-6299

Glossary

Accounts payable — the amount of money *known* to be owed (i.e., unpaid invoices that have been recorded) to vendors and suppliers that have provided goods or services to an organization.

Accounts receivable — money owed to a nonprofit for services rendered or goods provided on credit.

Accrual accounting — a method of accounting that recognizes economic events regardless of when cash transactions occur. Economic events are recognized by matching revenues to expenses at the time when the transaction occurs rather than when payment is made or received. Accrual accounting is generally required because it shows a more reasonable expression of the true state of an organization's financial position than does the **Cash method of accounting**.

Accrued liabilities — the amount *estimated* to be owed (i.e., invoices that have not yet been received and recorded) to vendors and suppliers that have provided goods or services to the organization.

AICPA — American Institute of Certified Public Accountants, the professional association of the accounting industry.

Assets — everything of value that an organization owns. It can include both tangible and intangible property, such as cash, stock, inventories, real estate, furniture and equipment, property rights, accounts receivable, or goodwill.

Audit — an examination of records and financial accounts to determine their accuracy and produce financial statements that fairly reflect the true financial status of an organization.

Auditor — the person, usually a Certified Public Accountant, conducting an independent audit for an organization.

Average payment period ratio — measures the average time that elapses before the organization's current liabilities are paid.

Bad debts — accounts receivable that are uncollectible or of doubtful collection.

Bad-debt expense — a statement of activities account that includes credit sales that are uncollectible.

Balance Sheet — see **Statement of Financial Position**.

Balanced scorecard — an integrated set of measurements assisting an organization in keeping track of its outcomes as compared to its goals. It utilizes four performance measures — financial perspective, customer perspective, internal perspective, and learning and growth — to help monitor and improve an organization's level of effectiveness.

Benchmarking — compares ratios, trends, and analyses (both financial and nonfinancial) of a nonprofit with those of its peers, and measures an organization's results against its best-performing peers.

Bond — a certificate of debt issued by a government or corporation to raise money for an organization.

Budget — a detailed annual financial plan that anticipates and projects both revenues and expenses of an organization.

Capital expenditures — funds that are used to acquire long-term assets, such as buildings, land, equipment, etc.

Capitalization — converting an expense into an asset; it spreads the cost of an asset over the length of time of its usefulness. **Capitalization of a fixed asset** converts an expenditure into a fixed asset, based on the dollar value and useful life of the asset.

Cash — assets in the form of currency, or **cash equivalents** that can be easily and quickly converted into currency.

Cash method of accounting — a method of accounting that records revenues when they are received instead of earned, and expenses when they are disbursed instead of incurred. Revenues are not matched with expenses.

Cash/current — generally includes cash in bank accounts, cash equivalents (anything easily convertible to cash within one day, such as money market accounts), and certificates of deposit (if less than 365 days to maturity).

Cash/noncurrent — generally includes cash designated for capital replacement and acquisition that is invested in longer-term assets (such as Treasury bills or bonds) and trustees' investments (cash set aside from bond proceeds to be used in capital projects), with maturity expected to be greater than 365 days.

Contribution — a gift or an unconditional, nonreciprocal transfer of assets to a nonprofit. Contributions may be in the form of cash, stock, bonds, art, property, or any other tangible asset that has value; qualified nonprofit 501(c)(3) organizations may accept contributions from individuals, other nonprofits, or for-profit corporations, for which the donor may take a tax deduction.

Current ratio — measures an organization's liquidity, or how readily the organization is able to pay off all its current liabilities.

Days cash on hand ratio — measures the number of days of average cash expenses that the organization maintains. The ratio can be expressed in terms of either days cash on hand in short-term sources or in all sources.

Days in accounts receivable ratio — measures the average time that accounts receivable are outstanding (also known as the average collection period).

Debt service coverage ratio — measures the ability of an organization to pay back its long-term debt by comparing its bottom line cash with its annual debt service payments (principal + interest expense).

Depreciation — the process of allocating (amortizing) the original cost or fair market value of a long-term tangible asset over its estimated useful life.

Depreciation expense — an expense deduction on the statement of activities arrived at by allocating (amortizing) a defined part of a long-term asset over its estimated useful life.

Disclaimed opinion letter — see **Opinion letter**.

Expenses — the resources expended to run the operations and programs of an organization.

Fixed assets — tangible property with a long-term useful life, such as land, land improvements, buildings, building equipment, movable equipment, furniture, leasehold improvements, or capitalized leases.

Footnotes (also referred to as **notes**) **to financial statements** — addenda to the financial statements. Some are required by GAAP, such as the first footnote on all financial statements, which is a summary of significant accounting policies used in the creation of a nonprofit's accounting books and records. Additional notes may be used to describe the nonprofit's programs, investments and investment policies, affiliated organization investments, property and equipment, lease commitments, contingent liabilities, long-term debts and leases, joint cost allocations, related party transactions, pension plans, temporarily and permanently restricted assets, and any significant subsequent events.

Form 990 — the informational tax form that must be filed annually with the IRS by most nonprofit organizations that have applied for tax exemption and have been approved by the IRS under Section 501(c)(3). It is a public document, available for inspection.

Fundraising expenditures — expenses incurred in the solicitation of contributions and grants from individuals, foundations, government agencies, and others.

Fundraising ratio — measures the efficiency of a nonprofit's fundraising programs by comparing the amount spent on fundraising to how much it receives in contribution and grant revenue.

Generally accepted accounting principles (GAAP) — a basic set of principles, standards, and procedures prescribed by the American Institute of Certified Public Accountants that attempt to achieve uniformity in the way that nonprofits display their finances. They are a combination of authoritative rules and generally accepted ways of reporting and recording financial information.

Generally accepted auditing standards (GAAS) — the rules that CPA auditors must follow when performing an independent audit.

Grant — an award or contract received by a nonprofit from a foundation, another nonprofit, a corporation, government, or other entity.

Income Statement — see **Statement of Activities** below.

Interest expense ratio — measures the overall average percentage interest rate being paid by the organization to finance its debt.

Interest income ratio — measures the overall average percentage earnings on all of the organization's assets that have the potential to be invested.

Liabilities — everything an organization owes, the sum of its debts and obligations. **Current liabilities** are those that are due to be paid within 365 days. **Long-term liabilities** have a due date beyond 365 days.

Management and general expenses — expenditures on general oversight and management (except for direct conduct of program services or fundraising activities), general record keeping, budgeting, finance, and other general and administrative activities. Also included are expenses that are categorized as indirect, shared, or overhead — those that are essential to program administration but are difficult to allocate to specific programs.

Management letter — a letter that an independent auditor may issue with the audit report if there are significant issues of concern to the auditor uncovered during the audit.

Net assets — the difference between an organization's assets (what it owns) and its liabilities (what it owes). It is the accumulation of all the organization's financial surpluses since it came into existence (the equivalent of retained earnings on a for-profit balance sheet). Assets can be unrestricted as to their use or time of use. Or they may be restricted assets, as when a donor puts limits on their use. The restriction can be either temporary (if the restriction can be met either with the passage of time or by the purpose being fulfilled), or permanent (if the restriction never expires and cannot be removed).

Net margin — see **Net assets**.

Net (or total) margin ratio — measures profitability based on all revenues, including non-operating revenues. This typically means investment income is included, although it is generally classified as non-operating.

Non-operating revenues and expenses — revenues and expenses that are not related to a nonprofit's programs or mission, such as gain or loss from the sale of invested assets.

Nonprofit Audit Guide — periodically updated collection of generally accepted accounting principles (GAAP) and other authoritative guidance, as they apply to nonprofit organizations' accounting. Issued by the AICPA.

OMB Circular A-133 — a publication of the U.S. Office of Management and Budget prescribing audit requirements for nonprofits with government contracts.

Operating margin — the excess or deficit of revenues over expenses.

Operating margin ratio — measures profitability by comparing an organization's bottom line (the excess of support and revenues over expenses) to its total revenues.

Opinion letter — produced by an organization's external auditors at the conclusion of their review of the year-end figures, it expresses judgment on whether the management-prepared financial statements are "presented fairly" in accordance with GAAP and accurately reflect the financial status of the nonprofit. A ***clean opinion***

letter indicates full compliance with GAAP. A ***qualified or adverse opinion letter*** is a judgment by the external auditor that he believes that an organization's financial statements are not in compliance with GAAP. A ***disclaimed opinion letter*** is a judgment by the external auditor that he is unable to form an opinion on a nonprofit's financial statements due to incomplete information provided by management.

Permanently restricted assets — see **Net assets**.

Plant ledger — a subsidiary ledger of the general ledger, where all the elements for each individual asset are recorded, such as the asset's description, original cost, date of acquisition, annual depreciation expense, and accumulated depreciation.

Pledge — a written or oral agreement by a donor to make a contribution to a nonprofit organization. A promise to pay.

Private inurement — in the nonprofit context, financial benefits paid to a nonprofit organization "insider" (director, officer, senior manager).

Program services expenses — expenditures, goods, and services used in activities to fulfill the purpose or mission of the organization.

Program spending ratio — measures the proportion that a nonprofit is spending on programs to achieve its mission by comparing spending on management and general plus fundraising, to its spending on programs.

Qualified or adverse opinion letter — see **Opinion letter**.

Quick ratio — measures the organization's ability to meet short-term obligations from its most liquid, or quick, assets. It compares assets that are quickly and easily convertible into cash (such as cash, cash equivalents, and accounts receivable) to the organization's current liabilities. (Also known as the asset-test ratio.)

Ratio analysis — a method for taking two or more informational elements and utilizing them together to obtain additional information. Financial ratio shows relationships between raw data in the financial statements, usually expressed as percentages.

Reserves — surplus of funds available for unexpected circumstances.

Restricted assets — see **Net assets**.

Return on net assets ratio — measures profitability based on net revenues by comparing a nonprofit's excess of support and revenues over expenses to its unrestricted net assets.

Revenue — income derived by a nonprofit from providing goods and services and from other earning opportunities.

Sarbanes-Oxley (SOX) Act of 2002 — a law enacted to ensure that publicly traded for-profit companies have processes and controls in place to produce timely, fair, and accurate financial reports for boards and shareholders. It regulates audits and auditing processes to ensure board objectivity and auditor independence. Two provisions (whistleblower protection and document destruction) apply to nonprofits.

Statement of Activities (also known as the **Income Statement**) — a compilation of all revenues and expenses of a nonprofit organization; it also shows the excess or deficit of revenues over expenses and the change in net assets.

Statement of Cash Flows — reports the sources and uses of the organization's short-term cash and cash equivalents for the period concurrent with the statement of activities. It is a summary of where the organization's cash came from and how it was used.

Statement of Financial Position (more commonly known as the **Balance Sheet**) — represents and displays all of an organization's financial assets, liabilities, and net assets at a snapshot in time, usually the end of an accounting period (month, quarter, year), and conforms to the following equation: assets = liabilities + net assets.

Statement of Functional Expenses — displays all income and expenditures according to their primary functional classifications, such as program services, management and general expenses, and fundraising.

Support — income derived by a nonprofit from contributions and grants.

Temporarily restricted assets — see **Net assets**.

Trending — the display and analysis of data or information over time.

Unconditional promises to give (also known as **pledges receivable**) — contributions to a nonprofit that have been promised or pledged, but not yet received.

Unrestricted assets — see **Net assets**.

Suggested Resources

BoardSource. *The Nonprofit Board Answer Book, Second Edition: A Practical Guide for Board Members and Chief Executives.* Washington, DC: BoardSource and Jossey-Bass, 2007. The second edition of this best-selling, indispensable resource contains 80 questions and answers — a wealth of information about board structure and process, meetings, board composition, orientation, board-staff relations, financial management, and much more. The book offers insight gained from hundreds of board self-assessments and questions and challenges from thousands of nonprofit leaders. Written in an easy-to-use question-and-answer format, it includes action steps, examples, and worksheets.

Butler, Lawrence M. *The Nonprofit Dashboard: A Tool for Tracking Progress.* Washington, DC: BoardSource, 2007. Dashboard reports communicate critical information to your board in a concise, visual, more compelling way. Dashboards help nonprofit leaders focus attention on what matters most in their organizations. This book, for board members and senior staff, presents different options for creating dashboards and offers detailed illustrations and considerations. To help organizations get started with their own dashboard reports, the accompanying CD-ROM includes a dashboard generator file with two different customizable dashboard templates and how-to instructions for working with the file.

Fry, Robert P. *Minding the Money: An Investment Guide for Nonprofit Board Members.* Washington, DC: BoardSource, 2004. *Minding the Money* will introduce your organization to the current investment world of hard-won dollars and will involve nonprofit board members in investment planning in a non-intimidating way. With action questions, helpful tips, and real-life case studies, readers will understand difficult financial concepts they can implement in their own board service. A customizable CD-ROM offers practical appendices, including sample policies, self-guided investment audits, and Web links to applicable state statues.

Lang, Andrew S. *Financial Responsibilities of Nonprofit Boards.* Washington, DC: BoardSource, 2003. Provide your board members with an understanding of their financial responsibilities including an overview of financial oversight and ways to ensure against risk. Written in non-technical language, this booklet will help your board understand financial planning, the IRS Form 990, and the audit process. Also included are financial board and staff job descriptions and charts on all the financial documents and reports, including due dates and filing procedures.

Lawrence, Barbara and Outi Flynn. *The Nonprofit Policy Sampler, Second Edition.* Washington, DC: BoardSource, 2006. *The Nonprofit Policy Sampler* is designed to help board and staff leaders advance their organizations, make better collective decisions, and guide individual actions and behaviors. This tool provides key elements and practical tips for 48 topic areas, along with more than 240 sample policies, job descriptions, committee charters, codes of ethics, board member agreements, mission and vision statements, and more. Each topic includes anywhere from two to 10 sample documents so that nonprofit leaders can select an appropriate sample from which to start drafting or revising their own policy. All samples are professionally and legally reviewed. Samples are included on the CD-ROM.

McLaughlin, Thomas A. *Financial Committees*. Washington, DC: BoardSource, 2004. Accountability is increasingly important to nonprofits, and every board must be engaged in understanding its fiduciary duties. Learn about the core responsibilities finance, audit, and investment committees can hold. Discover how these committees can address challenges in helping the rest of the board understand complicated fiscal issues. This book will also help finance committees to stress the importance of board member independence in oversight and audit functions, and prepare the board to address potential new legal regulations.

About the Author

Steven Berger is president of Healthcare Insights, LLC, which specializes in the teaching and consulting of health care financial management issues. Healthcare Insights also created and sells INSIGHTS, a decision support management accountability software system tool that is used to streamline budgeting, improve monitoring, and enhance reporting. Prior to his role at Healthcare Insights, LLC, Mr. Berger was vice president, finance for seven years at Highland Park Hospital in suburban Chicago, Illinois. Before Highland Park Hospital and since 1978, he has been a hospital/health system finance officer in New York, New Jersey, and Missouri.

Mr. Berger has many years of health care financial management experience. He holds a Bachelor of Science degree in history and a Master of Science degree in accounting from the State University of New York at Binghamton. He is a CPA and a fellow of the Healthcare Financial Management Association (FHFMA) where he has served as president of the First Illinois Chapter. Mr. Berger is also a fellow of the American College of Healthcare Executives (FACHE). He has presented many health care finance–related seminars throughout the United States and Canada, including several two-day classes: Fundamentals of Healthcare Financial Management, Turning Data into Useful Information, Hospital Financial Management for the Nonfinancial Manager, Creating and Guiding the Information-Driven Hospital, and The Zen of Budgeting. He has also presented board-level financial training for BoardSource at its annual meeting.

Mr. Berger has written several articles on health care financial and general management issues that were published in *Healthcare Financial Management* magazine, including an April 2002 column on management accountability. He is the author of two hospital/health care financial management books. *Fundamentals of Healthcare Financial Management*, first published in 1999 by McGraw-Hill and the Healthcare Financial Management Association, is written from a practitioner's point of view and is a distillation of Mr. Berger's many years on the inside of health care institutions. The third edition of the book was published by Jossey-Bass (www.josseybass.com) in January 2008. Additionally, Mr. Berger is the co-author of *HFMA's Introduction to Hospital Accounting, 4th Edition*, which was published in the summer of 2002 by Kendall Hunt. In 2005, Mr. Berger wrote *The Power of Clinical and Financial Metrics*, which was published by Health Administration Press (www.ache.org).

Finally, Mr. Berger served a term as president of the board of Turning Point, a 501(c)(3) nonprofit community mental health agency. It is the experience that led to the creation of this book.

Additional information on training, consulting, or management accountability software (operating and capital budgeting, position control, balanced scorecard, labor productivity, monitoring and measuring goals through automated e-mail alerts) can be obtained at www.hcillc.com or e-mail at sberger@hcillc.com.